The Holistic Life

Sustainability through permaculture

ISBN: 978 1 86476 437 6

Axiom Australia

www.axiompublishing.com.au

Printed in Malaysia

The Holistic Life

Sustainability through permaculture

Ian Lillington

AXIOM

Acknowledgments and thanks

This book has been written in our own permaculture-inspired home in South Australia and 'on the road' in Australia, England and Wales, staying with permaculture and family friends. I'd like to thank all the hard working and inspiring people I have met (in person and through the internet) around the world over the last 15 years, each trying in their own way to live in the solar economy.

Like many permaculture books, this one has had a long gestation. I am grateful to all the staff at Axiom Publishing, especially John Gallehawk, Martin Cook and Greg Willson for their patience and good faith. Thanks to Richard Telford for the graphics that accompany the permaculture principles, Jan Sands for the colour illustrations, and to claire fulton and Russ Grayson for proof reading and peer review.

I'd also like to thank my family: Jo, Rowan, Ned and Gabriel, who with me, are part of developing our own permaculture lifestyle and who are part of the experiment to see if sustainable living is possible.

In 1989, Su Dennett and David Holmgren at their permaculture hub in the cool climate of central Victoria helped me realise that Permaculture was for me too, and they have continued to support my efforts in so many ways, especially by making available resources for use in this book.

Thanks also to: Patrick Whitefield in Somerset, England, for 'Permaculture in a Nutshell,' an early inspiration; Stephen Nutt in Devon for access to his extensive library and a quiet time to use it; Graham Bell and Nancy Whitehead, in Coldstream, Scotland, who bothered to put on a regular Permaculture Design Course in the early days of British permaculture, where I did my PDC in 1990.

Photographs by Adam Lee and Ian Lillington, except:

Page 9: Stuart Roper
Page 17: Susan Forth
Page 18, 45, 100, 111, 133: David Holmgren
Page 84: Jo Middleton
Pages 89, 103: Annemarie Brookman
Pages 91, 93: Russ Grayson

Garden Designs:

Page 57: Franck Savarton & Associates
Page 92: Virginia Sheridan

Last but not least, to my parents in Bristol, England who supported us on our trip in 2001-02 and who brought me up to be able to appreciate the good things about living sustainably.

And to you, the reader: if you have heard a little about permaculture, and want to know more, this book is for you. If you are an absolute beginner, this book is also for you. I hope it will lead you to find other people who are like-minded—the best thing about permaculture, for me, is the people I meet through it.

Contents

About this book

The first part of this book, based on the ethics of permaculture, describes an ideal that we can work towards. It covers what's wrong with the current environmental situation and why we need permaculture's holistic approach. The middle section provides practical short-term techniques that can be applied to 'buy time' as we deal with the huge environmental crisis we are mixed up with. It is based on what people are already doing in towns, cities and on properties around the world. The final part is a set of principles you can apply to choices in any aspect of your life. These underlying principles include a review of David Holmgren's permaculture principles, published January 2003. David was co-author of the original Permaculture book and has been developing and refining this new approach over the last seven years.

In this book 'Living Permaculture', I have emphasised the human role in sustainable living. We already have the technology to build a passive solar house, grow food, or make a composting toilet. What we don't know (yet) is what it is like to run a suburb, or a city with millions of people, in a sustainable way.

This book was written in an energy efficient house, in the time available between growing food in our garden and working in the local community. It was written on a secondhand computer with a first rate spell checker, and has been written with lots of local support—including a LETS member who services my computer and the friends and colleagues who have proof read it.

Most of the examples in this book draw directly from projects and research already known to me, or those I have been involved in. This book illustrates permaculture from our own family perspective as well from a more general outlook.

This book is a starting point, and gives a brief overview of a big subject. In writing a short book, I have tried to maintain the integrity of permaculture concept, and focus on the underlying principles, adapting them to any situation. The book is for any reader who wants to reduce personal use of fossil fuels and increase self-reliance within their local community. I would encourage the seeking out of other books I refer to, and find workshops, courses, local groups and individuals who will help explain what sustainable living is and how to work towards achieving it.

Central to this book is the need for people to work together, for without goodwill and co-operation, all our technical achievements are wasted. Permaculture is an approach to designing sustainable human habitat, and it starts with an ethical foundation (see page 24). It seems far too often we don't learn the lessons of history, but there are as many examples of people working together as fighting each other. Unfortunately, the latter tends to get most media coverage.

There has never been a more important time to work together, to concentrate on constructive change, and to put the earth first when we make our choices and decisions.

Ian Lillington
Willunga, South Australia, July 2006

Foreword

Ian and I were both part of the generation which through the late 1970s and early 80s, marched, shouted, and in a multitude of ways alerted the world to ozone depletion, acid rain, global warming and diminishing natural resources. We stood up and acted to save remnant forests, stop uranium mining, apartheid, and the insanity of the cold war.

We were labeled lunatics and hippies... We cried out, 'NO!' Many of us became depressed from reading newspapers, watching TV and gleaning impressions about the sorry state of the world.

Permaculture gave us, and many others, a way to say, 'YES!' It supported, encouraged and gave guiding principles and ethics to work for change and positive solutions anywhere we saw a problem.

Ian walks his talk. He has created with his family, a living, working, easily-replicable example of a more sustainable way of living. He advocates deep and lasting change in our world. Sustainability around the whole globe, not just in our individual backyards, but in every backyard, every farm, every city apartment and office block. He calls on each one of us to become part of the solution rather than part of the problem, and gives many examples and ideas of how this can be done.

Most importantly, Ian encourages and inspires us to work together for change. Permaculture, with an emphasis on community living, positive communication, empowered individuals, support and networking, helps create a sustainable basis for rapid change in our world view.

A major shift in the consciousness and actions of the western world is required, as many speakers and authors are repeatedly saying. There are no labels of lunacy any more. Even my twelve-year old son's state school projects call on him to think of solutions to the environmental and ethical problems of our world.

May this book find its' way into many, many hands and may each and every person awaken to the need and potential for personal and global transformation through sustainability.

Robin Clayfield,
Crystal Waters, Queensland

David Holmgren, Robin Clayfield and Ian Lillington at the Australian Permaculture Convergence, Eltham, Victoria, 2005

Terminology

The word 'permaculture' is a hard-working one—it has many uses! It is a decribing word (as in 'a permaculture magazine'), a noun (as in 'my block is a permaculture') and a verb (as in 'I do permaculture'). It comes from the words PERMAnent agriCULTURE, which is necessary if we are to have a permanent culture. It means that to sustain a permanent population on the earth we have to live within the energy available from the sun and the resources provided by the earth. I use a lower case 'p', as I think of the word 'permaculture' as like the word 'agriculture' or 'architecture'.

Part One:
Living permaculture—living sustainably

"What permaculturists are doing is the most important activity that any group is doing on the planet." David Suzuki

David Suzuki opening the Willunga Farmers' Market. Farmers' markets have blossomed over the last few years as one example of meeting our basic needs from local suppliers

Change and choice

We make choices every day. The choices we make are very powerful —the combined effect of many millions of choices makes a huge difference. By using ideas and guidance from permaculture principles and practice, you can choose to increase the chance of human survival and the survival of the other species of planet earth.

People in every country live as if the earth was created just for them. Very few people question whether it is right to use up resources and cause pollution in the way we do.[1] Whether it is right or not, it is dangerous—most people in 'developed' countries now rely on 'high tech' systems to provide all of their water, food and fuel.

This is a fragile and dangerous situation—a relatively small loss of oil production capacity as a result of Hurricane Katrina (in August 2005) had a big effect on oil prices. A hot summer in North America in 2003 meant days with no electricity in many cities. In 1998 and 1999, an explosion at a refinery in Victoria left two states of SE Australia without gas supplies for weeks; fear of the cryptosporidium or giardia bug in a New South Wales reservoir left 3 million people in Sydney having to boil drinking water; a breakdown in electricity supply left Auckland's CBD with no power for a month. These are just small warning signs of worse to come.

There is plenty of evidence we are living unsustainably —about 20% of the world's population is using 85% of the world's resources, very rapidly. Even if there were unlimited supplies of energy, we are on a dangerous course, because plenty of energy simply drives the consumption of other precious resources. No one can be quite sure how long oil, gas, soil or forests will last, but we do know that the 'developed' world is causing pollution, climate change, psychological stress and, for the other 80%, poverty and death.

1. Daniel Quinn Ishmael Bantam, 1992, and John Wiseman *Global Nation? Australia and the politics of globalisation*, 1998.

But there are people who are questioning the dominant way of thinking. These people are working in many different ways, both practical and visionary, to show how it is possible to live within the earth's limits. It is possible and desirable to act as if all people and the rest of creation matters.

The popular view of permaculture is that it is about chooks, gardens and mulch. Permaculture is about developing a community where people, technology, and the natural world are linked into an integrated system for sustainable living.

Permaculture's principles and techniques guide many people who are acting and thinking differently. In this book I set out both the vision for a sustainable planet, and some of the methods we can use to get there. Our economic system is only part of the total environment. We have used up a lot of the 'capital' from our environmental reserves —fossil fuels, forests, fish, and clean water—but our 'business' (economic growth) is heading for bankruptcy, because it has been draining that capital rather than generating income.

Techniques such as re-using water or recycling bottles are helpful in the short term, but we must plan to use less water, less packaging, less petrol—that is less in total—as they are simply running out. There are plenty of alternatives, but we need to get serious about these, rather than living as if there was an unlimited supply of what we know to be limited resources.

Permaculture is an ethical design system guided by a set of principles. A permaculture-designed system is one that uses renewable resources for most of its 'capital', and one that generates forests, good soils, clean air, clean water and local healthy food as 'income'. Permaculture design can be applied to farms, gardens, buildings, business and community. The permaculture approach is two fold and simultaneous:

1. The big picture—a vision of an ideal way of running the world, based on solar energy running local, small scale systems that provide for our needs.

2. The practical methods—personal, household and business scale choices that are not perfect, but heading in the right direction.

Both approaches require effort, they require change, and they require a different way of thinking, within a rapidly changing world, so why not make it change for sustainability?

Peak oil

We are around the time when we have used half of the world's total oil supply.[2] We won't run out immediately, but the gap between supply and demand is rapidly widening. Since the 1970s, advocates of permaculture have been promoting a way of living with our energy coming mainly from the sun, rather than from fossil fuels.[3]

The oil, coal and gas under the earth represent one billion years of stored sunlight. We have used around half of this in the last 100 years. Putting 500,000,000 years worth of stored energy into the atmosphere is a huge change, and a big challenge for Gaia, the living planet.

To many people sustainability implies that we maintain the same kind of lifestyle that most affluent people have at present, but really we are dealing with change to a world where concentrated energy is much less available to us. We have been dealing with big change for a couple of centuries, as we raced up a 'mountain' of energy. That experience of rapid change can help us as we start to go down the other side. These mountains or spikes occur in all natural systems, but this time we are at the top of a very big roller coaster of change, and there are going to be some catastrophes on the way down!

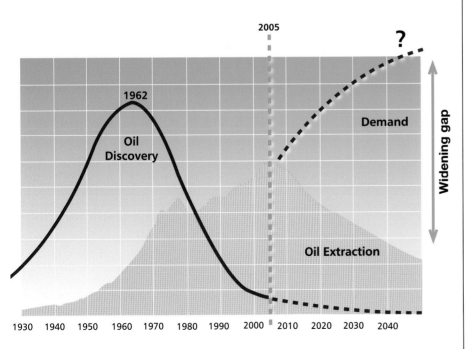

2 What is Peak Oil? Peak Oil is the simplest label for the problem of energy resource depletion, or more specifically, the peak in global oil production. Oil is a finite, non-renewable resource, one that has powered phenomenal economic and population growth over the last century and a half. The rate of oil 'production,' meaning extraction & refining (currently about 83 million barrels/day), has grown in most years over the last century, but once we go through the halfway point of all reserves, production will decline, hence 'peak'. Peak Oil means not 'running out of oil', but 'running out of cheap oil'. For societies built on ever-increasing amounts of cheap oil, the consequences may be dire. Without significant successful cultural reform, economic and social decline seems inevitable. (From the Energy Bulletin, www.energybulletin.net/primer.php).

3 Excellent information available at peak oil sites such as http://www.peakoil.net/; http://oilcrisis.com/ and see: The Party's Over, 2003 and Power Down, 2005 By Richard Heinberg, The Long Emergency, by James Howard Kunstler 2005, Beyond Oil, By Kenneth S. Deffeyes 2005.

Three starting points

Permaculture's principles and techniques can guide the way we see things and what we do as we move into this post-oil descent phase.[4] We can change the way we think and act as individuals much quicker than we can change the buildings of a town or change a field into in a food forest. Here are three simple starting points to help guide positive change:

1. Keep in touch with nature

At a practical and a spiritual level, we can only hope to live sustainably if our designs and choices are modeled on nature. Regularly spending time in a garden, forest, by a river or at the beach helps us understand the natural rhythm of life; which is our guide to sustainability. This is in contrast to much of modern life, where most of us are spending money seeking material answers to non-material needs.

2. Spend your money locally

When you spend money with a local business and on a local product or service, you keep that money cycling within your local economy. You may be paying a bit more in the short term, but the only sustainable way to meet your needs is from local sources, so support your local baker, bee-keeper, mechanic, builder and anyone else who meets your needs locally.

3. Use less fossil fuel

Your level of fossil fuel use is a measure of the environmental destruction you are causing. Petrol, gas, oil, and electricity derived from those sources is very powerful, attractive, seductive stuff. But the use of those fuels, directly in cars, homes and businesses and indirectly in most of the food and goods we buy, is very destructive and polluting. It's better to run out of oil slowly, giving time for transition, than to burn it up quickly. It's also a good idea to practice using less fossil fuel, as it always gives us a better environment, even if we don't run out.

4 H. T. Odum and E.C. Odum,
The Prosperous Way Down, 2001.

Without Trucks
Australia Stops

Even the trucking industry recognises how dependent we are on a single fuel source!

A story

"Life is the first gift, love is the second, and understanding the third." - Buddha

"Once there was a people who were active and successful. They had machines and technologies to make their lives easy and they had time to think. In their sky were three bright stars—forming a triangle, and the triangle shape dominated their design—all their geometry, machines and devices had three sides or three points. This was a fine, strong, shape, but perhaps a bit spiky, rigid and a little limiting? The philosophers amongst these people wished for a bit more variety, and a new challenge.

Then, unexpectedly, a fourth star appeared in their sky—as bright as the other three, and close to them. New possibilities of shapes began to occur, and the foremost thinkers of this people began to talk about a new geometry—at first the square, and then the cross. The more radical among this people began to talk about the circle, (but how could a circle come from four points, asked the more conservative?)

Gradually, their lives were transformed. A whole new way of looking at things developed. There were so many possibilities, though only one new point had been added. These people adopted the new way of seeing, became wise, generous and co-operative and went on to live sustainably for many generations."

A new day dawns filled with hopes and possibilities

A different way of seeing the world

Permaculture is a different way of seeing the world. When you think of a garden you may see roses, fruit trees or vegetables—or you may see a complex interacting ecology. When you think of a house you may see an opportunity for saving (or for wasting) resources. When you consider more than six billion people on a finite planet you can see a population disaster, or a great resource for creativity.

How about thinking of these 6 billion as one million towns each with 6,000 people. That seems a lot more manageable to me. Imagine our cities as a group of 'towns' of around 5,000 to 10,000 people where most of the needs of that 'town' are met by the people of that 'town'. When people get their food and other needs from local sustainable sources they are part of the sustainable solution we need…and don't forget our existing towns and villages can already meet many of their needs.[5]

Permaculture is a different way of approaching all aspects of life. It's an approach guided by principles, yet it is practical in its application. This is a challenging way of thinking, but one that is badly needed if we are to manage the planet in a way that allows us and our children to survive, and allow the rest of nature to survive as well.

> "Never doubt that a small group of committed citizens can change the world. Indeed it is the only thing that ever has."
>
> Margaret Mead

5 Bill Mollison *Permaculture—A Designers' Manual*—Tagari 1988. See chapter 14 – Strategies for an Alternative Nation.

Delegates at an International Permaculture Convergence in Sweden, from more than 60 nations and all continents

Smart design

Whenever we need to do something, anything, we can do it in a way that creates more or less benefits and creates more or fewer problems. How do we choose to create more benefits? For example, we need light in our living spaces. We can design and build houses that let in plenty of natural light without letting in too much summer heat or losing too much heat in the winter. We can choose to get up at daybreak and go to bed soon after dark instead of getting up about 3 hours after daybreak and going to bed around midnight.

We will need some additional light. If we choose a low-energy globe we save energy (good for the environment) and we save money (good for us) over the lifetime of the globe. But we need to reduce the amount of electricity we need to levels that can be generated from local sun, wind and water sources.[6]

Everywhere we must focus on understanding what the problem is, and be imaginative about what we can do about the problem—and it can be done at a personal and household scale.

Demand-side management

At a larger scale, a power generation company can either choose to build a new power station, or can have people reduce their demand. There is a huge cost to building a new power station. There is a small but significant cost to buying a low energy globe. A few progressive power companies around the world have brought these two factors together and *given* their customers low energy globes (and/or sold them other low energy appliances at low cost). By doing this, the power company has avoided the cost of building a new power station—a huge financial and environmental cost. Building the light globe factory takes perhaps 1% of the energy involved in building the new power station.[7] This is an example of 'demand side management', known about since the 1980s, but not often a strategy by water or power supply companies, unless things get desperate—they are worried that they will end up selling less water or electricity.

So solve one problem and solve others at the same time. Thinking and designing in this way is a big challenge and one that needs an understanding of what the real problems are.

6 Bill Mollison, *Permaculture—A Designer's Manual*, 1988. See pages 24-25, where the industrial and permaculture eggs are compared. The permaculture egg system still needs some dense energy to smelt iron, but at a level that can be produced from renewable resources. All the other needs of the chickens are met locally.

7 Paul Hawken, Amory & Hunter Lovins propose this approach in *Natural Capitalism* and *Factor Four*. While these are thought-provoking analyses, they continue to promote economic growth and increased wealth, albeit in a more natural way. They don't show what energy sources are going to power these 'high-tech' and 'green' scenarios, whereas permaculture's low tech systems can certainly be powered by the sun using known technologies.

Meeting new challenges

New challenges are constant and all around us. We humans have a huge impact on the earth and we must manage this more sensitively. Every day the cities of the world take in millions of tonnes of food, water and goods, sending out millions of tonnes of waste. This is seen as good for business but business (the economy) is a 'wholly-owned subsidiary' of the environment. You can't have a business at all unless the environment is in good condition. There are limits to what we can take, process and throw away.

The Gaia concept[8] has become more widely known over the last 20 years and helps us understand our role as part of the living earth with finite resources. Although we won't immediately solve all the problems this is a good time to try new ideas. We have the resources and knowledge that give us a chance to experiment. Through good design, a permaculture-inspired approach avoids doing unnecessary work, which of course creates further pollution. Instead it does what is necessary by using resources that are local and sustainable; especially the energy of the sun converted into food, timber, medicine and fibre by the action of plants.

Permaculture is an ethical design process for a sustainable lifestyle. It uses methods gleaned from everywhere to create a 'toolkit' for sustaining life on earth. It is grounded in the basic laws of nature and in common sense.

8 James Lovelock and Lynn Margulis *Gaia; A New Look At Life*, 1979.

Permaculture is about helping people make real and lasting change in the way they live. This is a time of rapid change—let's make it change for the better!!

This book includes a personal story—our family story—a story of change from being a couple with no children and living in England to a family with three children in Australia. Although a big geographical change, this book is primarily about our journey towards living sustainably—and exploring what it means to live holistically—taking into account the wider consequences of our actions. This journey has been guided by the wisdom of the people we have met through permaculture and ideas contained within permaculture's ethics and principles. All of which are outlined in this and other mentioned books.

Our experiences described come from 15 years of aiming to live sustainably in Australia, and many years' previous experience as activists for social and environmental change in the UK. I have aimed to make this book relevant to the widest audience possible, but I only know for sure that it will work for my culture —the white 'western' [affluent] world of the 21st century.

Over the last 10 years, we have acquired a house, a car, a garden, a mortgage and a business [called 'Living Permaculture']. These are pretty normal acquisitions for a family living in a wealthy country at the turn of the millenium. However, by choice, we have progressed through this material world with as little negative environmental impact as possible.

Jo, Ned, Rowan, Gabriel and Ian

- We have one car where most similar families have two or more. We use bicycles, buses and trains for many of our journeys.

- We have both designed and built a house using low energy materials, and where we can live comfortably on less than half the electricity an average rich world family uses.

- We have a mortgage around half the average for a new family home owner, which helps us spend at least twice as much time at home. More time with our small children and working in the garden— which in turn further reduces our living costs.

- This is one example of applied permaculture —good design to reduce environmental impact—and provide positive feedback. The more time we spend at home (rather than elsewhere working for someone else), the smaller our bills become, because we increase time available to meet our own needs and decrease the costs of commuting. A simple and very effective strategy.

The value of a working example

There have been many analyses over the last 40 years of what is wrong with our modern way of living in terms of its impact on the environment.[10] The world needs many examples of how we can have a good quality of life without ruining the planet on which our life depends.[11]

We set out to build a home, garden and lifestyle that was a working example of how to have a low negative impact on the environment. Australia has the sun, the land, the resources and the people who can be a living demonstration of sustainability.

Many people here are committed to living more lightly on the earth, and yet, at the same time, Australians are the biggest polluter, per person, in terms of carbon dioxide emissions and the second highest user, per person, of water.[12]

New examples of permaculture are created each year, and now there are people practicing permaculture in almost every country of the world.[13]

The essence of permaculture is ancient in origin—it starts with the civilizations of the world which have survived for thousands of years—including the indigenous peoples of Australia, Africa, Asia and the Americas. However, permaculture is a modern integration of many skills and disciplines, brought together to design ways of living sustainably in the 21st century.

"In the last several decades a growing number have been exploring a simpler way of life. Without major media coverage to mark it's progress, the growth in simpler ways of living has emerged largely unnoticed in many developed nations. Quietly and without fanfare, people have been developing ways of living that touch the world more lightly and compassionately..." [9]

Energy efficient design of houses (often called passive solar), and solar hot water are two cost-saving and simple ways to live more sustainably

9 Duane Elgin, Voluntary Simplicity, 1981.

10 see amongst others, Meadows et al *The Limits of Growth* 1972; and *Caring for the Earth - A strategy for Sustainable Living* 1991 from IUCN & UNEP & WWF.

11 For one summary of just how bad things are, see John Ralston Saul's *The Unconscious Civilization* - Chapter 1 called The Great Leap Backwards. Also very useful for understanding the global picture is New Internationalist magazine - www.newint.org.

12 John Archer—*Australia's Drinking Water*—Pure Water Press, 2001.

13 see Permaculture International website www.permacultureinternational.org/global directory.

Permaculture solutions

In a desperate quest to own and consume, people get stressed, and an otherwise stable society breaks down. Many people feel vaguely uncomfortable, and others actually ask: "with all our technology, information and resources, surely we can have a safer, saner world than what's currently around us?"

We need to think about going down the mountain.

Permaculture's solutions are driven by a desire to actively work towards a safer, saner world, that is a nicer place to live right now, as well as being a place where future generations can live. But the solutions are challenging, as they involve a change of thinking from constant growth to managed reduction.

1. Planning the descent

Instead of constantly striving to climb to new heights, we need to think about going down the mountain.

The last 300 years, and especially the last 50, have seen a huge growth in human population, based on a parallel exploitation of the earth's natural resources—fossil fuels like oil, coal, gas and natural resources like fish, forests and topsoil. Politicians and economists call this economic growth and it's generally considered to be a good thing, especially if you want to get re-elected to government or stay at the top in business. Up to a point, this is natural—every group of plants, animals, or bacteria do the same —when there is plenty of food and energy the population grows rapidly.

However, growth never continues indefinitely. Either a population uses up all the resources that have given it the chance to grow and the population collapses again; or it moves on to a new set of resources and continues growing. Humans, over the last few generations, have always been able to find new resources, but there are many indications we have already passed the point where new resources are available. We live on a planet with finite physical resources, but we do have incoming solar energy a lot of human ingenuity using the sun and these resources we can sustain human life.[14]

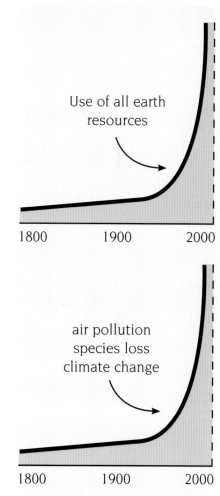

14 The website www.hubbertpeak.com is a good source of more information both on the peak of oil extraction—about now —and the alternatives. It gives equations comparing solar versus oil energies. For example, it shows the sunlight that reaches the earth every 24 hours is more than the total oil that has been extracted and still available.

15 H & E Odum A *Prosperous Way Down —Principles and Policies*, Wiley 2001.

Living in the affluent countries of the world during the last three centuries has been about living in a world of constant growth and change. It is like climbing a mountain—lots of energy is needed and new tasks have to be achieved with every step. At the top of the mountain, you have to find your way back down. This can often be the more dangerous part—especially if the options are clouded by mist and rain![15]

In the last 100 years, the human population has suddenly accessed a huge amount of oil, gas and coal, and experienced an unprecedented period of growth. On the graph (page 19) most people have been going up the steep side of the mountain. Climbing up has been hard work, competitive and energetic. Being at the top it is exhilarating (we can see the whole world from up here), but also dangerous (which way down, is it steep, or is the weather going to change?)

It is now time to adapt—fossil-fuels are declining and the descent needs to be planned. This 'descent' to a lifestyle based on less fossil fuel energy can be chaotic, or using permaculture principles, it can be graceful and creative. If you're a bike rider, all the work of getting up the hill is towards the prospect of a good descent! Only one thing is certain, we can't go up for ever. We won't have this abundance of oil and gas again, so we need to plan differently.

While the sun goes on shining (probably for millions of years) we have a great source of energy, but it comes in a different form to the concentrated supplies of oil, gas and coal. We have been living in a fossil fuel economy. Now we need to adapt to the solar economy by converting sunlight into the things we need.

2. Converting the sun into what we need

The best way to convert sunlight into something we can use is by growing plants—and humans have been doing this for a long time. Perennial plants are especially useful, as unlike wheat, rice, maize & potatoe, they need little labour or fossil fuel in tractors. Hence the perma(nent) in perma-culture.

Not only do humans have a lot of experience in growing plants, plants have had millions of years to perfect the process of photosynthesis —trees naturally turn the fairly dilute energy of sunlight into food and energy for themselves and wood, fruit, medicine, fibre etc. that we can harvest.

Using the sun

There are enough studies showing how much solar energy is available to us, and how little we use it. Although solar hot water, passive heating of houses and photo-voltaic cells are options, a simple, low cost starting point is to allow plants to do the work for us. They are sophisticated converters of sunlight, with millions of years' experience.

By using permaculture principles, we will inevitably design and create environments full of useful plants, which in turn will help the human population find ways down the mountain, or at least a plateau, where we can stabilize and assess new options.

Permaculture practitioners, over the last 30 years, have set out to show how living in a system powered by sun (the 'solar economy') rather than oil (the 'fossil fuel economy' is the logical alternative). There are plenty of societies which have done this for centuries, and we are fortunate to have experience of both traditional peoples' and modern experiments in living within the solar economy.

Food gardens promote healthy eating by providing positive experiences of the fun and pleasure of growing, preparing, and eating good food. This is a far more effective way of encouraging a lifelong joy in healthy eating than dry information about vitamin content and prescriptive diet pyramids.

Urban food gardens provide practical solutions to negative environmental impacts of commercial food production. Bringing food production closer to home reduces its ecological footprint by cutting down 'food miles'—the energy used to transport produce over hundreds or thousands of kilometres, from growers to processors to retailers to people's tables.

People of all ages and abilities can garden. Raised beds can be provided for those who are less mobile. Gardens are a place where everyone learns something—about plants, nature and our place in the scheme of things. Gardeners develop and test locally appropriate, sustainable growing methods that may be used on a much greater scale.

From claire fulton's report,
The Contributions of Community
Gardening to Health Promotion

CANH South Australia, 2004

As we convert from a fossil fuel economy to a solar one, we need an ethical approach, (which you could call wisdom, rules or guidelines).

Care for the earth: even if we become proficient at using the sun's energy, we need to be careful with all the other resources of the earth—as we need more than energy. Forests, fish, good soil, minerals, and many other raw materials.

Care for people and **share surpluses**: abundant solar energy is useless unless there is a healthy living planet for plants and animals including humans!

These permaculture ethics are described in more detail on the following pages

16 However many researchers and governments are quietly but firmly acknowledging the limits to easily accessed oil. The Melbourne Age, 22 April 2006, editorial: www.theage.com.au/news/editorial.

3. An ethical approach

Limits to growth—the precautionary principle

There are some who argue despite all the evidence, we can go on growing, and contend there are always new sources of energy and material to be used. It's true there are often 'false peaks' as you climb a mountain—you think you can see the top, but when arriving, all you see is yet another higher peak. It may be that the next part of the way 'up' is for humans to find ways to settle new planets, perhaps new galaxies, but at present this could only happen by using a huge part of the earth's remaining fossil fuel and other resources. In doing so all the problems we see at present would dramatically worsen.

Permaculture practitioners may be accused of lacking boldness in declaring that we are at the top of the mountain. Some say that a combination of technologies including micro-chips, nuclear fusion, genetic modification and human ingenuity can allow growth to continue indefinitely[16]. It's true that times of chaos lead to all kinds

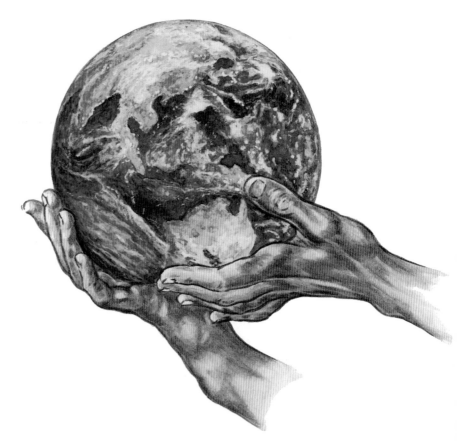

The blue-green planet that we call the Earth—"It's the only one we've got"

of innovation, but I don't see any reassuring models leading to 'high energy sustainability' where technical fixes will solve all our problems.

Even if we do continue to develop these exciting and dangerous areas, bordering on science fiction, it would be wise to secure our future through stabilizing the earth's population and provide a secure livelihood for everyone. This can happen by limiting consumption in the affluent world, addressing distribution of resources and getting beyond a growth economy mentality. Put another way, if this approach is wrong, we are still alright. If the high consumption approach is wrong, we are in big trouble!

This is sometimes called the precautionary principle, and it is both an ethical and conservative approach—as in conserving the things we need.[17] The technical answers are already known. What is required is the will to make it happen and incentives (or positive feedback) to help people make real and lasting change. (see principle #3—Obtain a Yield page 120).

Permaculture's ethical motivation comes from a sense that we know this 'mountain' (our life support biosphere—sometimes called Gaia). We know we are at the top, because our 'maps' tell us.

We know we have done all the economic growing that we need to. Instead, we need to grow a lot of trees, as permaculture shows that perennial plant systems are the only sustainable way to convert sunlight into products that we need for food, fibre and medicine and shelter.

Many people are in tune with the following thoughts, expressed by Robert Hart,[18] who spent his life developing ethical and sustainable projects. He reminds us to always think positively. He writes: "With our present knowledge, there is no technical reason why every woman, man and child on Gaia's earth should not be adequately fed, clothed, housed and given the opportunity for self realisation. In the history of human evolution, a new species is appearing in many parts of the world—a species endowed with the mental, moral, and spiritual qualities fitting it to co-operate with Gaia's self-healing capacities. It would be positive to call the new species Homo altruisticus."[19]

"With our present knowledge, there is no technical reason why every woman, man and child on Gaia's earth should not be adequately fed, clothed, housed and given the opportunity for self-realisation."

"In the history of human evolution, a new species is appearing in many parts of the world—a species endowed with the mental, moral, and spiritual qualities fitting it to co-operate with Gaia's self-healing capacities. It would be positive to call the new species Homo altruisticus." [19]

17 *Permaculture: A Designer's Manual.* Bill Mollison 1988. Page 507, paragraph on conserver societies.

18 Robert Hart was a British-based author, researcher on agroforestry, gardener who developed a food forest in Shropshire. He lived from 1913 to 2000.

19 Robert Hart *Beyond the Forest Garden* 1996.

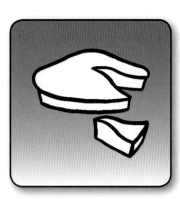

Ethics

Permaculture is an ethical design process for a sustainable lifestyle.

Until recent generations, each society had its own set of rules, or ethics, which directed a way of that society sustaining itself—often for thousands of years. Only with the industrial revolution did a new rule book come along—based on exploitation of large amounts of the earth's resources and using fossil fuel to run this new system.

Mollison and Holmgren, in researching the early permaculture idea, observed a similar ethical basis to every traditional society.

Like design principles, ethical principles were not explicitly listed in early permaculture literature, and since the development of the Permaculture Design Course, ethics have generally been covered by three broad maxims or principles:

- Care for the Earth
- Care for People
- Distribute Surplus, Set Limits to Consumption and Population

These principles were distilled from research of community ethics as adopted by older religious and cooperative groups. The third and even second ethical principles can be further seen as derived from the first.

Ethics and principles for everyday life

Although we might argue about the precise definition of 'sustainable', it is clear that we are not living sustainably now. One common thread that truly sustainable cultures have is that they are based on an ethical approach to life—for example only to hunt or harvest certain foods at certain times. This ensures there is plenty for next month, next year or next generation.[20]

In the book *Introduction to Permaculture*[21], Bill Mollison says: "the permaculture ethic pervades all aspects of environmental, community and economic systems. Co-operation, not competition is the key."

Graham Bell, Scottish permaculture author and activist develops this theme: "I believe all religions and codes of conduct stem from the needs of people at given times and places. One of the great

20 see Robert Lawlor's *Voices from the first day*, 1991, and other works by Lawlor.

21 Bill Mollison with Rene Mia Slay, *Introduction to Permaculture*, 1991.

beauties of the Islamic culture is that it is not a religion but a way of life. In Christian Europe, our understanding of mathematics, geometry and astronomy and consequently our ability to build and navigate, were greatly enhanced by absorbing scholarship from the great thinkers of Islam. Science, beauty and God could never be perceived as separate, but as different aspects of the unknowable infinite.

"Permaculture is not a cult or religion—it is a system for designing which can be adapted to any culture or place... We all have the same interest at heart—survival—looking after each other is of paramount importance."[22]

We live in times of rapid change—this is a good time for positive change. A good place to begin change is with yourself—so think ethically!

Living permaculture means getting more than one benefit for each of your actions, including the action of spending money. At present, so many of our activities are done for a single purpose and cause environmental damage as a side effect. Instead, a local, integrated approach to life has many benefits, and far fewer negative effects.

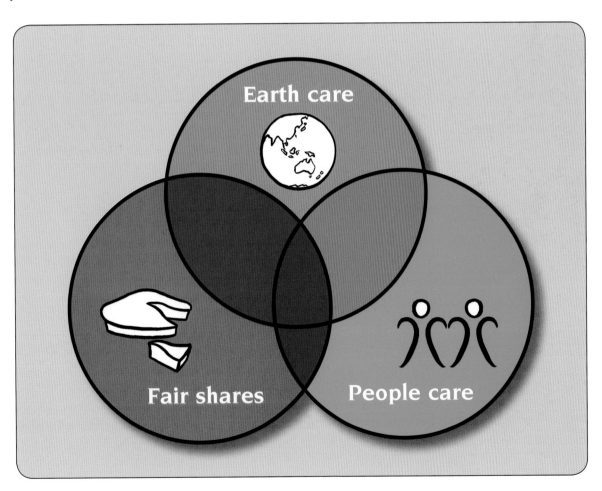

22 Graham Bell, *The Permaculture Way*, 1992.

A brief history of permaculture

The word permaculture was originally a blend of permanent and agriculture. However, it is increasingly used to mean permanent culture. Throughout history, civilizations have collapsed when they over-reached their food supplies, and left deserts in their wake. Are we about to do the same?

The 'traditional' starting point for newcomers to Permaculture is a book called *Introduction to Permaculture* by Bill Mollison with Reny Mia Slay. The *Introduction to Permaculture* is an amalgamation and revision of *Permaculture One* (the original book) and *Permaculture Two*, with additional chapters. This book; *The Holistic Life* aims to make accessible the best of permaculture from the last 30 years, and develop the people-centred approach to permaculture, which has steadily grown alongside permaculture's original land-based approach.

Whether it means culture or agriculture, permaculture has always focussed on natural systems, especially forests, because they are self-sustaining.

If we are to have any chance of sustaining human life, we have to replicate natural systems and use good design to create our own systems. These systems have to encompass social and economic systems that sustain us, as well as systems that produce our food, fibre, timber and clean water and air.

The scientific basis of permaculture comes from both natural systems ecology (an ecological approach to agriculture) and from thermodynamics. David Holmgren's work, (and this book), is significantly influenced by the work of Howard Odum and the need

David Holmgren

Bill Mollison

to understand energy—where we get it from, how we use it, and what happens once we have used it. In particular, we need to better recognise our current and almost complete reliance on fossil fuel energy, which is both polluting and finite.

The essence of permaculture is ancient in origin—taking inspiration from the civilizations of the world that have survived for thousands of years—including the indigenous peoples of Australia. However, permaculture is an integration of many skills and disciplines, brought together to design ways of living sustainably in the 21st century.

The early concept (in the 1970s) was a combination of ecology, landscape and agriculture. David Holmgren and Bill Mollison collaborated on the original permaculture concept in the 1970s in Tasmania, with David as student and Bill as lecturer. Under Bill's guidance, David's graduate thesis became the main body of the book *Permaculture One*. This book showed how ecology and agriculture could be combined, by conscious design, to create a landscape filled with sustainable food production systems.

David Holmgren describes that time in an article on Radical Origins of Permaculture:[23] *"Permaculture arose from interaction between myself and Bill Mollison in the mid 1970's. We were two (very different) social radicals on the fringes of (different) education institutions, at the global fringes of western industrial society in Tasmania.*

Bill Mollison as bushman turned senior tutor, in the Psychology Department. of the Tasmanian University, attracted large student audiences to hear his radical and original (pre-permaculture) ideas while outraging the academic establishment.

I was a student in the Environmental Design School, a revolutionary "experiment" in tertiary education at the Tasmanian College of Advanced Education. This design school ran for ten years under the inspired leadership of Barry McNeil, a Hobart architect and education theorist. Visiting and local professionals accounted for a substantial part of the staff budget. There was no fixed curriculum but a strong emphasis on decision making processes and problem solving. Self assessment, democratic organization and many other elements which radicals within tertiary institutions only dream about, were reality within the school.

Even within the intellectual freedom and stimulation of Environmental Design, I was on the fringes, with my all consuming permaculture work and my student-mentor relationship with Bill Mollison. My work was largely ignored within Environmental Design although Barry McNeil has since acknowledged it was probably the most important concept to emerge from the school."

By the mid 1980s, Bill Mollison was roaming the world, on a shoe string budget, teaching Permaculture Design courses—a minimum of 72 hours of intensive study, in the classroom and outside—where instant food gardens were created from whatever materials came to hand. This travel and teaching led to the publication of Mollison's 580 page book, *Permaculture— A Designers' Manual* with Reny Mia Slay and Andrew Jeeves in 1988. The *Designers' Manual* advocates a strong ethical and social dimension to permaculture and remains the 'Bible' for serious permaculture study.

Meanwhile, David Holmgren and partner Su Dennett were developing their demonstration property 'Melliodora' in central Victoria and publishing a series of books on designing and creating permaculture buildings and landscapes. David has recently produced a *Collected Writings 1978 – 2000*[24] and new look at permaculture principles in *Permaculture: Principles & Pathways Beyond Sustainability*.

Colin Endean has his face painted by Aboriginal Elder Bobby Brown for the celebration at the end of a Permaculture Design Course

23 & 24 Collected Writings 1978-2000 see www.holmgren.com.au.

Fellow travellers

The consumer society means using up billions of tonnes of resources in a non-renewable way. It is almost all a one-way process—from rainforest, mine or paddock, and then to the dump, after these goods have been used for a minute, an hour or perhaps a few years. Ted Trainer's book *The Consumer Society*[25] and other works by Trainer show clearly how economic growth is unsustainable and how we need to move to a 'conserver society' using permaculture principles and techniques.

This approach to sustainable living doesn't have to be called Permaculture—there are many 'fellow travellers' who recognise this common ground.

These include:

- Home birth, Homoeopathy and herbal/traditional medicine

- Personal growth, self healing

- Home schooling, Steiner/(Waldorf) and other 'alternative' schools

- Community gardens, city farms and 'subscription farming'/community supported agriculture/food box schemes

- LETS and ethical investment

- Use of legal structures for community ownership of land

- Bio-regionalism, spirituality of place and indigenous cultural resurgence

25 Ted Trainer "*The Consumer Society*" 1995, (Zed Books, London) and see also Ted's webpages - http://www.arts.unsw.edu.au/tsw/.

The permaculture 'flower' has seven petals, showing the interlinked nature of seven 'domains'. Ethical and design principles are at the core, while a specific design, or the design of permaculture systems in general, spiral outwards.

Around the edge are listed a selection of fellow travellers; why not add your own?

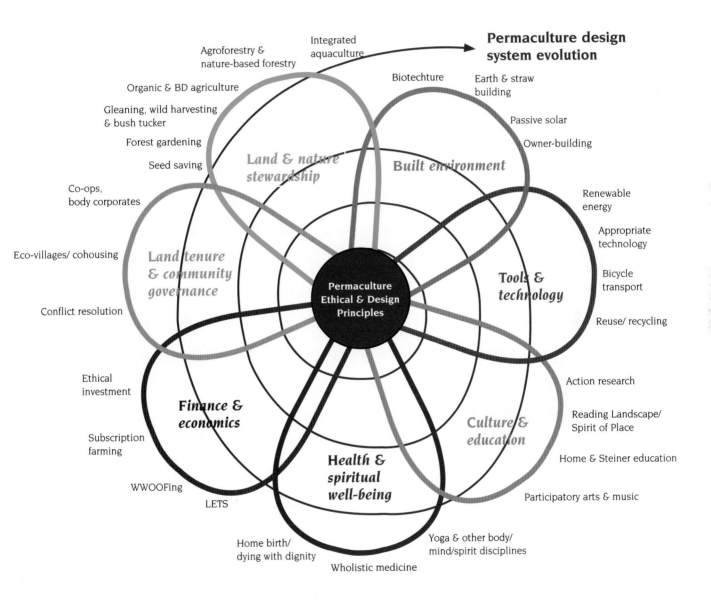

Permaculture flower used with permission of David Holmgren.

Overflowing rubbish bins are only one sign of an over-consuming society

Adelaide's Christie Walk Eco-City project

26 www.ceres.org.au.

27 www.urbanecology.org.au.

Permaculture—an antidote to consumer society

Permaculture is more than a gardening system, but exactly what it is varies from person to person. For many people (who may or may not garden), it is about how they meet their needs from local sources and contribute no waste to the environment. It is possible to live in a small flat in the inner city with no garden and yet live with little damage to the environment. It is also possible to live on 10 acres in the bush, with a desire to live sustainably and yet do a huge amount of environmental damage.

There are now many well established examples of permaculture-designed properties and lifestyles, though it may take 10 years to create a well established system based on perennial plants!

However, a 'low impact' lifestyle can be developed in just a few days —in the 'inner city' or in the bush. But a lifestyle doesn't usually get rated as a demonstration project! Perhaps that too is changing, as people seek out simpler solutions and quality, not quantity, in their lives.

Most people in the rich countries of the world live in highly urbanised societies. They are within 20 kilometres of a business centre. Most of these people expect to drive their own car from place to place, and to have unlimited food available through supermarkets. Their high consuming habits have detrimental effects on the fields, forests and oceans supplying their needs.

However each city also has many people who turn this dense living to their advantage and minimise their negative impact. Melbourne's CERES environmental project[26] and Adelaide's Christie Walk Eco-City project[27] provide many useful ideas and examples of low-impact city living. Living in the city increases the possibility of walking, cycling, recycling, reusing and generally reducing the needs of each person, but the pressures to consume seem greatest as well.

Permaculture provides a set of ideas (and ideals) which have inspired people across the world for 30 years. These are people who dare to question dominant "consumer thinking". Amongst other things, permaculture provides moral support for like-minded people who dare to ask confrontational questions like, "do you really need a car?"

To question the need for unnecessary consumption of material goods, let alone to strive to consume less, seems to be quite threatening to most people in a society where the dominant thinking is that this consumption is healthy, good and strong. There's lots of evidence that we are heading for disaster, environmentally and socially, yet most people carry on the same as before.

There is also room for optimism—perhaps we are part of a new renaissance where good sense will prevail over human greed —certainly promoters of permaculture continue to show how there can be enough for everyone's need. Meanwhile more people consume more non-renewal resources everyday. What is worse, generations of affluent people now exist who have no experience of walking as a way to get from A to B, or mowing grass by hand, let alone eating something they have planted, nurtured and harvested.

Is this really a problem? After all, we have been hearing for at least 30 years that "unless we do this or that, we'll be in a bad way by the year 2000". Well, many of the problems that were foreseen have occurred, and many people feel that the quality of their life has decreased[28].

But most people try to shut out the gloom and doom, and/or believe that minor modifications, like an improved recycling service, have dealt with the environment problem. After all, we still have plenty of food and a comfortable lifestyle, don't we?

Yes we do, but most people in Australia and other 'rich' countries continue to be cushioned from the worst effects of our consumption. Governments, transnational companies and their associated media operations like to portray problems in Darfur or the Middle East (and hundreds of other areas of destruction and suffering) as isolated incidents, the result of some unconnected, local conflict. Really, they are the results of struggles for power over resources —especially materials like oil which is exploited to fuel more consumption of non-renewables.

What we consume here is inextricably linked to what happens in the rest of the world—our high consuming lifestyles have a big knock-on

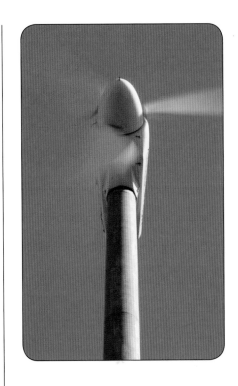

Wackernagel and Rees and others have emphasised that if everyone lived at the standard of industrialised countries, it would take two additional planets comparable to Earth to support them, three more if the population should double; and that if worldwide standards of living should double over the next 40 years, twelve additional "Earths."

For more on eco-footprinting see page 106.

28 See page 34.

effect. Magazines such as *New Internationalist*, *Resurgence*, *The Ecologist*, and others clearly and consistently illustrate this better than I can within a short chapter.

Debates about what is a sustainable population for the rich countries of the world become meaningless when you understand these links. Such countries could double population whilst halving the resources we currently use.[29] Does this seem impossible? Many older Australians grew up with 50,000 litres of water per family per year. Now water supply companies allow for up to 500,000 litres per family per year. This picture of ten-fold increase in consumption is repeated over and over, with every item or service we use.

Consumerism equals waste, unless we design systems making use of the 'waste products' in another part of our system—hence the permaculture principle #6, 'Produce No Waste'[30]. Most of our towns and cities have a land-fill problem. Most people have a household space storage problem. More shops are open for longer hours, more goods are sold, more ends up in landfill or storage. So much food has never been available before, and poses an interesting evolutionary situation—one in five rich world children are considered obese. Have you considered that it might be desirable to buy and consume less? But even if you want to, how do you get off the treadmill?

Gleaning

In rural and urban areas, gleaning has become a way of life.[31] Originally it was the right of poor people to gather corn in the fields after the harvest. 21st century gleaning is a necessity for some who need to scavenge just to eat, and an ethical pastime for others who abhor the waste of good food or materials.

Rich world suburbs have an officially sanctioned hard rubbish collection. Residents pile up unwanted goods on the side of the road and after a few days or a week the council will remove them. Meanwhile, it is an invitation to reuse a great wealth of resources.

Hidden costs

Producing our consumer goods causes pollution and destruction, but most of this is unseen—it happens elsewhere. What's more, our economies are struggling, despite what 'market analysts' might like us to believe, because it is more and more expensive to exploit the diminishing areas of fuel, forest or fish that were once available in abundance.

29 *Habitat - Journal of the Australian Conservation Foundation*, Vol 33 #2, April 2005, called 'Population? No problem'.

30 See page 126.

31 *The Gleaners and I*—an excellent and unusual film made in 2000 by French film director Agnes Varda.

Meanwhile, an average 20 tonnes of rubbish per person goes to the dump each year. Unbelievable? Well, this rubbish is made up of one tonne in the weekly household refuse collection, and around 10 times this as a result of waste from all industries producing the cars, white goods, buildings and services we use. For Australia, that's 19 million people multiplied by 20 tonnes. If you do a similar calculation for the populations of North America, Japan and Western Europe, you will get to a figure of billions of tonnes of waste per year.

Why do we carry on damaging our life support system?

A relatively few people are making a lot of money, in the short term, out of this process of high consumption. Perhaps they are using it to try to create a safe haven for when/if the environmental 'Armageddon' comes—perhaps it is an addictive drive to get more and more, indefinitely. But however rich you are you can't sustain life for ever on a planet devoid of its beautiful ecology of living oceans and living forests.

Most people in the 'rich world' are getting employment out of this consumption and destruction, though that's not usually obvious. They (we) are not becoming millionaires, but earn enough to have food, a decent house and the chance of some luxuries like travel, alcohol, and some leisure time if all goes well.

People in these two categories, the rich population of the world, accounts for only about one-sixth of the global population. Many of the other five-sixths of the world's population are under huge pressure, just to stay alive. Increasingly they are giving up relatively sustainable peasant lives in villages to move to cities, partly pushed out by 'progress', partly hoping to make money by moving from peasant to consumer lifestyles.

It seems to be an increasingly mad world. If you feel like saying "stop the world, I want to get off!" then read on. The following chapters are for you!

"When it became definite that India would attain independence, a British journalist interviewing Gandhi asked whether India would now follow the British pattern of development.

Gandhi replied 'It took Britain half the resources of the planet to achieve this prosperity. How many planets will a country like India require?'"

Our quality of life peaked in 1974—It's all downhill now

By George Monbiot

The Guardian, UK

January, 1, 2003

With the turning of every year, we expect our lives to improve. As long as the economy continues to grow, we imagine, the world will become a more congenial place in which to live. There is no basis for this belief. If we take into account such factors as pollution and the depletion of natural capital, we see that the quality of life peaked in the UK in 1974 and in the US in 1968, and has been falling ever since. We are going backwards.

The reason should not be hard to grasp. Our economic system depends upon never-ending growth, yet we live in a world with finite resources. Our expectation of progress is, as a result, a delusion.

This is the great heresy of our times, the fundamental truth which cannot be spoken. It is dismissed as furiously by those who possess power today—governments, business, the media —as the discovery that the earth orbits the sun was denounced by the late medieval church. Speak this truth in public and you are dismissed as a crank, a prig, a lunatic.

Capitalism is a millenarian cult, raised to the status of a world religion. Like communism, it is built upon the myth of endless exploitation. Just as Christians imagine that their God will deliver them from death, capitalists believe that theirs will deliver them from finity. The world's resources, they assert, have been granted eternal life.

The briefest reflection will show that this cannot be true. The laws of thermodynamics impose inherent limits upon biological production. Even the repayment of debt, the pre-requisite of capitalism, is mathematically possible only in the short-term. As Heinrich Haussmann has shown, a single pfennig invested at 5% compounded interest in the year AD 1 would, by 1990, have reaped a volume of gold 134bn times the weight of the planet. Capitalism seeks a value of production commensurate with the repayment of debt.

Now, despite the endless denials, it is clear that the wall towards which we are accelerating is not very far away. Within five or 10 years, the global consumption of oil is likely to outstrip supply. Every year, up to 75bn tonnes of topsoil are washed into the sea as a result of unsustainable farming, which equates to the loss of around 9m hectares of productive land.

As a result, we can maintain current levels of food production only with the application of phosphate, but phosphate reserves are likely to be exhausted within 80 years. Forty per cent of the world's food is produced with the help of irrigation; some of the key aquifers are already running dry as a result of overuse.

One reason why we fail to understand a concept as simple as finity is that our religion was founded upon the use of other people's resources: the gold, rubber and timber of Latin America; the spices, cotton and dyes of the East Indies; the labour and land of Africa. The frontier of exploitation seemed, to the early colonists, infinitely expandable. Now that geographical expansion has reached its limits, capitalism has moved its frontier from space to time: seizing resources from an infinite future.

An entire industry has been built upon the denial of ecological constraints. Every national newspaper in Britain lamented the "disappointing" volume of sales before Christmas. Sky News devoted much of its Christmas Eve coverage to live reports from Brent Cross, relaying the terrifying intelligence that we were facing "the worst Christmas for shopping since 2000".[my emphasis] The survival of humanity has been displaced in the newspapers by the quarterly results of companies selling tableware and knickers.

Partly because they have been brainwashed by the corporate media, partly because of the scale of the moral challenge with which finity confronts them, many people respond to the heresy with unmediated savagery.

Last week this column discussed the competition for global grain supplies between humans and livestock...

There is no doubt that a rising population is one of the factors which threatens the world's capacity to support its people, but human population growth is being massively outstripped by the growth in the number of farm animals. While the rich world's consumption is supposed to be boundless, the human population is likely to peak within the next few decades. But population growth is the one factor for which the poor can be blamed and from which the rich can be excused, so it is the one factor which is repeatedly emphasised.

It is possible to change the way we live. The economist Bernard Lietaer has shown how a system based upon negative rates of interest would ensure that we accord greater economic value to future resources than to present ones. By shifting taxation from employment to environmental destruction, governments could tax over-consumption out of existence. But everyone who holds power today knows political survival depends upon stealing from the future to give to the present.

Overturning this calculation is the greatest challenge humanity has ever faced. We need to reverse not only the fundamental presumptions of political and economic life, but also the polarity of our moral compass. Everything we thought was good—giving more exciting presents to our children, flying to a friend's wedding, even buying newspapers—turns out also to be bad. It is, perhaps, hardly surprising that so many deny the problem with such religious zeal. But to live in these times without striving to change them is like watching, with serenity, the oncoming truck in your path.

Guardian Unlimited/Guardian Newspapers
http://www.guardian.co.uk/

Part Two: Living permaculture

By simple orientation towards winter sun, solar hot water and use of low impact building materials, these houses are both comfortable and sustainable. Within walking distance to buses, shops and schools, their occupants have low fuel bills and are not car-dependent

Permaculture is two things simultaneously. It is a 'discipline' with a set of ethics and principles—used in the way we might practice yoga, shiatsu, meditation or the wisdom of a religious leader or spiritual guide. It also has practical means for achieving a move towards sustainable living. In both senses, it is something to be incorporated in all aspects of a healthy, caring and thoughtful approach to life.

Earlier sections of the book show how we need to get much better at using the sun's energy, especially via plants, to help us travel down from the 'oil peak' in a safe and prosperous way. The following section covers some of the main techniques you can use or adapt for your journey down the mountain.

Permaculture as a toolkit for sustainable living

Growing food locally is an important part of permaculture, but permaculture is much more than this. It is a set of values and techniques to be incorporated into every part of your life, and a way of living as part of your community. You may live in the city or country, you may be young or old, new to the area or someone whose family have lived in your area for many generations. Through permaculture, you can develop a better sense of place that will help you meet your material and spiritual needs from the local area.

Permaculture designs are a success if they help us use less non-renewable resources. For example, recycling your grey water is useful, but not very useful if you continue to be a very high water user. A permaculture-designed system will both recycle water and allow you to use less water in total. Recycling your bottles and cans is useful, but if you consume more each week, recycling is only helping reclaim a small part of the resources you have used. A permaculture-inspired system, with more food in your garden, home brew in the cellar and preserves in your pantry, means you will need less bottles and cans in total—perhaps none!

Reducing our eco-footprint

Even if we access sustainable fuel sources, it is important to change our high-consuming habits, otherwise we will use up all other resources and continue to destroy the remaining living systems on the planet, including human life. In most countries in the world, native vegetation such as forest and hedgerow continue to be lost as large-scale agriculture pushes them out. Everything we consume has a knock-on effect elsewhere. Unless supplied locally, our requirements for food, transport, building materials and every other service damages the environment somewhere else.

Although there are many new trees being planted through Landcare-type initiatives, these don't compensate for trees being lost each year through land clearing, let alone replace the trees cleared over the last two centuries. In the UK, where there is a greater area under trees than at any time for centuries, many of these are 1990's community plantings (still young trees) or they are conifer plantations. Fifty-percent of ancient woodlands in northern Europe have been lost since the 1930s—and it is in these old forests that bio-diversity is to be found.[32] These huge and important areas of forest in our own countries don't just disappear—they have been cut down to make money from the wood itself and to make way for certain types of agriculture, usually high energy agriculture using fossil fuels to supply remote markets. Making money isn't a bad thing, but making it is, if at the expense of our lifeblood.

'Eco footprinting' is a simple starting point to assess your impact on the earth. You can work out your own 'footprint' online at www.myfootprint.org

Brick-veneer subdivisions like these take no account of orientation to get winter sun or cool summer breezes. Their occupants always have high electricity and petrol costs or else suffer from heat, cold and isolation

32 Woodland Trust, who have acquired over 1000 special woodlands in the UK to protect them. www.woodland-trust.org.uk.

Setting targets, measuring change

Energy is most obviously measured at the electricity or gas meter or at the petrol pump. But water use, and 'waste' leaving your home, office or factory, is also a form of energy and this can also be measured, at least in an approximate way.

In reading about the following methods, keep in mind the energy you use can be measured and targets can be set to improve (reduce) your fossil fuel use. The focus can be to make lasting changes to the way we act—not always an easy task!

To assess your household energy use begin with the following:

Metered energy use

Keep a record of your electricity (and gas) meter reading (not just the dollars on the bill). By comparing meter readings from quarter to quarter, you can assess whether you used more or less and what the reasons were. Water meters are easily read and are a useful tool to monitor resource use. Does usage increase every year? What would it take to achieve a decrease?

Unmetered energy use

- How many journeys are made by car? 100%? 50%? 0%?
- How many kilometres do you travel each year?

By knowing these figures you can begin to manage car useage, and, quite possibly, decide to reduce it. Anything can be managed the same way, that isn't metered. Some strategies are covered in more detail later in this section.

Socially responsible targets

Targets can be set about increasing the number of journeys made by foot, bike or public transport or reducing the overall number of journeys made.

Increasing the amount of time or money given to community projects or charities and the amount of time spent on campaigning for a better environment are two other areas some people measure and aim to improve year by year.

Rubbish as a measure of your eco-footprint

Do you put your rubbish bin out for a weekly collection? Is it full every week? The waste in your bin is a really good indicator of how much you are consuming (ie., wasting).

Set yourself a waste reduction target—perhaps, at first, put the bin out three weeks in four, then every other week, and then, once per month. By thinking first, and avoiding the buying of rubbish in the first place it can reduce the waste you throw away. This is an excellent way to reduce negative impact on the environment and it helps reduce the cost of rubbish removal—every time the bin truck doesn't have to stop means a cost saving for your local council.

You can do the same with recycling—a two-stage approach because a recycling bin is also a measure of consumerism. Of course, it is good to recycle everything you can, but aim to cut down the recycling frequency because a full recycling bin each week indicates unsustainable levels of consumerism.

Good as it is, recycling is still a high energy consumer—the materials have to be transported long distances for processing, and lots of energy is used in the reprocessing. It's better to reduce the packaging when a purchase is made (eg. fewer bottles and cans, more fresh food) Where possible reusing containers is an excellent way to help.

The audit approach

These suggestions can be seen as a kind of audit. Some local governments offer a home audit service to cover all aspects of living more sustainably.

"Audits are a great way of understanding in precise terms how a household uses energy and [a way] to make recommendations about what changes they could consider to reduce their energy usage. Audits within the home are a tremendous educational opportunity . . .

"There is also the potential to design the audit so that emissions [of greenhouse gasses] before and after the audit are recorded and emission reduction can be monitored."

My story

It's 23 years since I first heard of permaculture and 16 since I took a permaculture design course—the starting point for serious permaculture. At first I thought it was about herb spirals and tyre ponds, but gradually I came to realise that it was the linking thread or system that joined together all the problems I was concerned about.

As an 11 year old, I recall the first Friends of the Earth action—a delivery of thousands of non-returnable bottles to a company headquarters in London. As a teenager in 1974 in England, it was when I did my homework by candlelight during 'power cuts' (black outs) that I became aware of the fragility of energy supplies. I became concerned about loss of countryside as I saw the fields I played in get turned into housing estates. So at this influential stage of my life, I became conscious of the real limits to energy supply, to non-renewable resources and loss of countryside.

In 1979, I went to university to study geography, because I like maps, but quickly discovered it was probably the most holistic degree course there was. It showed me how a systems approach applies to both natural and human activity on the surface of the planet. During and after my time at university and in response to my concern about the environment, I volunteered on a number of city farms and was later employed to co-ordinate the establishment of projects to insulate the homes of people having difficulty paying their fuel bills. This led to an invitation to do similar work in Melbourne, Australia.

I had visited Australia in 1986 and seen permaculture projects in action, notably CERES in Melbourne. This led to a visit to the newly-built home of David Holmgren and Su Dennett in the hills of central Victoria.[33] Here I realised permaculture could be applied to a small property (one hectare or two acres), and in a cool climate, and was therefore relevant to northern Europe, North America and other situations and countries with a high population density.

After visiting permaculture-inspired projects in Botswana and Zimbabwe with my partner Jo, I finally got the message that permaculture was about applying good design in any situation—from window box to farm and from temperate to tropical climates.

33 David Holmgren Melliodora—the story of Hepburn Permaculture Gardens, 1995.

see www.holmgren.com.au.

In 1992, soon after the birth of our first child, we migrated to Australia and have been immersed in permaculture of some sort ever since. In 1997, we began our own permaculture demonstration project—a family home on a small block in the Willunga Garden Village in South Australia. (see case study at page 52).

Putting the culture in permaculture—a saner lifestyle allows time for music, gardening, and a healthy social life

A family way of doing permaculture

We hear the word 'sustainable' used a lot. In reality, most of us in the rich countries of the world are at best moving towards sustainability. When you hear the word 'sustainable' I suggest that, mentally, you substitute the phrase 'more sustainable'.

Our family's lifestyle is more sustainable than most, but it is still far from being truly sustainable. We still use a lot of fossil fuel, to undertake a lot of energy-dense activities—activities like driving, flying (occasionally) and eating food from the supermarket. In terms of our eco-footprint, it is our purchase of non-local food (about 25%) that causes most damage; because the foods have been transported long distances which consumes fuel, and because we are left with packaging to dispose of.

Developing a more sustainable lifestyle

The best location

Rather than the bush, we chose to live in a small town not too far from Adelaide. That's not difficult in Australia, where living 50km from the city means you are in the country.

The children go to school in town and amenities such as post office, shops, playgrounds and friends are within cycling or walking distance—even in the rain. If we have to go to the city, there are plenty of trains and buses.

House and land

We chose a small block—about 800 square metres (which is less than a quarter acre), to reduce time spent on maintaining the land—dealing with weeds, planting and so on. However, we also have access to the village's (one hectare, or more than two acres) of common land.

The house we built takes advantage of nature's resources as these are available in our village. In the winters, which can be quite cold (night temperatures between 5 and 10 degrees Celsius),

Our house from the road, with a wind break of locally-sourced casuarinas

Patio on the sunny side of the house, with shade from grape vines in full production

the house is heated mostly by sunlight. In the summer it is mostly the wind that keeps us cool.

We installed other energy (and money)-saving features, such as solar heated water, a pot-belly stove that burns any small diameter dry wood (rather than the so-called 'preferred woods' of mallee root or red gum, which are harvested at the expense of the natural environment) and a cool cupboard—an air-cooled pantry.

We conserve water wherever we can (to reduce the load on the reservoir and sewage system and as a matter of principle). A third tap in the kitchen brings in gravity-fed water from our rainwater tank. Our bath is next to the toilet so the used water, that is known as 'greywater', can be bucketed to flush the toilet.

Another thing we sometimes do is to pee in the garden (on the compost heap or on mulch around trees, not near edible plants) and we do not shower every day. Simply washing is sometimes all that's required.

Ballerina (miniature) apple trees produce lots of food from a small space. Netting keeps off birds

Firewood harvested from fallen branches and tree pruning, fully dried in summer sun, for heating the house and hot water in winter

Feeding ourselves

As much as possible, we eat from our garden, but because we cannot grow everything needed we source the rest from local suppliers such as the weekly farmers' market and the local dried foods co-op, which buys from local suppliers where possible.

Our local Farmer's Market is a great asset. It's less than a kilometre from home and the first in our state. The market, every Saturday morning, provides us with a choice of 25 producers who sell only local produce.

To further diversify the sources of our food, we swap surplus produce from our garden and work with our local permaculture group, providing mutual assistance in establishing gardens and orchards.

As a result of these activities, our family of two adults and three children use the following:

- About $1.20 electricity per day for all our needs (4 Kilo-watt hours per day)
- One 45kg gas bottle per year—supplying our cook top only
- One tonne of locally-gathered firewood per year
- 200,000 litres water per year for home and garden
- 6,000km per year by car for work
- 12,000km per year by car for all other purposes

We have:

- A mortgage of $100,000, repayable at a level that allows us to work part-time and spend the rest of the time with family or in our garden or community
- Smaller food bills—it is difficult to say how much—when we eat our own food, some of the money we save allows us to buy 'luxuries' like local—organic where possible—delicacies such as smoked kangaroo, organic olive oil, locally-made chutneys bread and organic wine
- Better health—we use homoeopathy and make few visits to GPs and hospitals. The public health service is a wonderful asset but

very expensive in terms of taxes and impact on the environment, so using it less often is another 'win-win' in our opinion.

Overall, we haven't done anything very difficult, or very different, except perhaps to buy a block of land in an eco-village. I believe we have made about 50% savings on what a normal Australian family consumes—with a gain in quality of life. People ask where we get the time to do some of these 'sustainable' things. While it is true that we are busy doing these things, it is also true that most other people are very busy too.

The challenge for becoming more sustainable is deciding what to do next—or, perhaps more accurately, what not to do next. Our next 25% of saving will be more challenging than the first 50%. But if everyone were to start by making the easier savings we would see a huge improvement and, maybe, meet the international targets for greenhouse gas emissions.

Quality rainwater from our own tank

Locally grown organic food can now be bought in supermarkets

34 David Holmgren, *Gardening as Agriculture*, article 7 in Collected Writings 1978 – 2000 CD Rom.

35 For many useful tips and articles, see *The Organic Gardener*, magazine from the ABC's Gardening Australia series.

36 *How To Grow More Vegetables Than You Ever Thought Possible On Less Land Than You Can Imagine!* J Jeavons, 1979 Ten Speed Press; and see also *Designing And Maintaining Your Edible Landscape – Naturally*, Robert Kourik, 1986 Metamorphic press.

37 Ken Fern *Plants for a Future*, 1997 and see Plants for a Future website, which has a searchable database of 7,000 plants. www.pfaf.com.

Growing your own

If each suburban garden were producing food or fibre, the whole city would become a kind of farm. Permaculturists, call this 'garden agriculture' and by re-directing the time and resources that go into maintaining ornamental gardens, high levels of local production could easily be achieved:

"By 'garden agriculture' I mean small scale intensive production systems associated with homes and primarily producing for human needs, although tradable surpluses might be produced. Human labour rather than machines provide the major power input."[34]

This chapter won't teach you how to garden. You only learn that by getting your hands dirty. This is to encourage you to 'get growing' with a few techniques and hints, and to point you to the wealth of other excellent resources.

The first part of this book showed why it is important to get our food from local sources—it is the only sustainable way. There is room in every garden for some annual vegetables. In a small area with good soil, a large proportion of the family's needs can be grown.[35]

Straight or wild?

There are two types of approach to vegetable gardens within permaculture systems—the intensive and the wild. The intensive system will probably use straight rows, lots of compost and winter crops planted as soon as the summer ones have been harvested. Yields can be very high. Because this kind of garden gets a lot of attention, the higher value crops like capsicum, egg plant, melons, tomatoes, carrots, brassicas, etc., can be very successful. (Jeavons[36], Kern[37] and others have experimented with these systems.)

The wild system is more like a miniature ecology—a combination of insects, birds, mulch, soil and plants that are (more or less) complementary in the way a natural ecology is. This is a very low input garden, but it can still produce good yields. It lends itself to high production of the 'easy' vegetables—basil, potatoes, zucchini, silver beet, broad beans, garlic, lettuce, pumpkins, sweet corn, parsley, and lemon grass.

Our veggie patch is mainly this wild system—because it gets very little attention between building, children, earning money etc. But it produces all of our garlic for a whole year and pumpkins and potatoes for quite a lot of the year. I have listed crops that I find easy—in any other area, or even in another part of my town, on different soils, you will have a different list. The important thing is to always grow what grows easily and then decide whether to grow the more difficult things.[38]

Many of these annual vegetables are self seeding—they drop seeds in situ or seeds like the pumpkin go through the compost and back to the garden next spring. As well as the annuals, the garden is a nursery for fruit tree seedlings—apricots, peaches, apples, loquats, and avocados pop up each year, having spent some time as seeds in the compost heap. These 'volunteers' are either left in place or transplanted to friends' gardens.

38 Michel and Jude Fanton, *The Seed Savers' Handbook* 1993 is a very helpful guide to what grows where and how to save the seed.

A market garden producing fruit, tomatoes and many other vegetables, less than 10km from a major capital city

Principles of passive solar design

Homes and offices can be designed to catch sun for the cooler half of the year and avoid solar gain in the hotter part of the year. Some simple design principles can be applied to any new building and are also useful when renovating an existing building.[39]

The aim is to reduce the use of fossil fuel while still having a comfortable environment. Perhaps it would be more comfortable as many people find air conditioning and gas heating a health problem, so natural alternatives are very desirable.

These approaches to designing and building are valid whether you are planning to be connected to mains services (ie mains electric, gas, water, sewer). or to run separate from these services

Terminology

- A house that performs well in summer and winter is called a passive solar house, and may or may not be connected to reticulated services.

- Active solar systems make use of devices such as pumps and fans —still better than using fossil fuels alone.

- A house that is not connected to mains services is called an autonomous house.

Passive solar design principles

Every new building, made from any materials, can meet passive solar standards by giving attention to:

1. Orientation

Choose a block that allows a long north* side to the house, to allow winter sun to come into the house.

You can make use of the different angle of the sun in summer and winter on the northern side. The sun will be at a low angle in the east and west during all seasons, but on the north*, the right dimension of eave overhang will give summer shade and allow winter sun into the house.

39 Useful references are:

N Hollo *Warm House, Cool House*, 1995 Choice Books and M Mobbs *The Sustainable House*, 1998 Choice Books.

The Autonomous House, Design And Planning For Sustainability, Brenda and Robert Vale, first published 1975, republished 2002.

The Integral Urban House, Olkowski, Olkowski and Davits *The Sierra Club*, 1979—despite being 30 years old, a classic book for sustainable urban living.

* north in the southern hemisphere, south in the northern hemisphere.

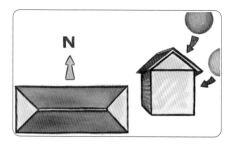

Additionally, deciduous vines on the north will enhance this effect. (see #4 below)

2. Insulation

The external walls and ceiling/roof must be insulated, and if the floor is not a solid slab, that needs insulation underneath as well. This is about creating a warm 'envelope' to live within. Insulating batts within stud walls, or rendered straw bale walls are effective insulators.

3. Ventilation

At night, or when cooler winds occur, it is necessary to be able to cool the house quickly by having plenty of cross ventilation. It is also desirable to have some sort of roof ventilation—so that hot air can be vented out. Easy opening and closing of windows/vents and good draught proofing are the main design requirements.

4. Integration of landscape and house

The most obvious example of integrating the house interior with the exterior environment is to use deciduous vines trained on wires on the north side to give summer shade. Grapes are ideal, as they have maximum leaf between November and April—the hottest months in most of Australia—May to September in the northern hemisphere.

5. Thermal mass

The slab and/or internal walls made from stone, brick or earth materials provide a mass that heats and cools slowly to provide heat retention in winter and 'cool retention' in summer. While the external walls can also be made of dense materials, these do gradually transmit the heat, so a solid brick, mud brick or rammed earth house will be slower to heat up in a heatwave but also slower to cool.

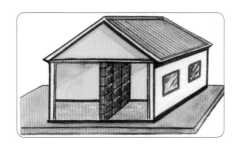

40 For unusual and excellent case studies see Tony Wrench *Building a Low Impact Roundhouse*, Permanent Publications 2000 (www.permaculture.co.uk) and David Holmgren *Melliodora*, Holmgren Design Services, 1996. (www.holmgren.com.au).

Applying the principles of passive solar building

The challenge and the fun of applying these principles is to get a balance of heavy and insulating materials in a form that suits the owner/user. It is possible to do much of the design work yourself and take your sketches to a building designer or architect to finalise the plans.

There are many human factors in house design and construction. So as well as getting the above principles right, think about:

Your own expectations:

• How big a house do you really need?[40]
• How far from services (schools, shops, health services?)
• What are the total costs in terms of time, energy and money?
• Can the space you enclose be multi-purpose?
• How long do you expect the house to last?
• How long do you expect to live there?
• Resources available

Consider:

• You and your family—how is your health, skills, time available? You could be involved in physical building work, or managing the work, or both or neither.

• Time—how soon do you need to move in?
  Is your scale realistic?

Can you start small and extend later? It is quite possible to build a house in stages, but it is better to plan the stages (at least in outline) from the start.

• Help—what is available from family, friends, LETS, (see page 81) and professionals?

• Fun—make the building process enjoyable and safe and simple. You can request your contractors throw old nails or sharp pieces of metal in a bin rather than in you future garden. Most contractors are quite reasonable about this if given advance notice. Our builder called it the barefoot building site concept, although you don't go barefoot on a building site, it should be managed as if you were going barefoot.[41]

- Money—to what extent can you support local businesses and local trades? (see Money section at page 81). How much can you use human labour in preference to mechanical? Human labour, if fed on local food, is a very sustainable resource and much less damaging to the environment than machinery.

Materials selection

Building or renovating will use some fossil fuel in the construction stage as well as when living there. Aim to reduce the long term energy running costs by wise use of energy during construction. Aim to build a house to last hundreds of years, where energy used now is not 'thrown away' when the house is demolished. Many modern houses are designed to be demolished within 50 years.

Some energy is used in backhoes, drills, electric saws etc., but much more is hidden (embodied) in the materials. Cement, for example, is a 'high embodied energy' material because it uses a lot of energy to produce it. Earth, by comparison, is a low embodied energy material. (see page 107)

Good design of house eaves allows winter sun to enter, while keeping summer sun out

41 Ian Collett, Stabilised Earth Constructions—pers. comm.

A permaculture house and garden—a working example (in Willunga, South Australia.)

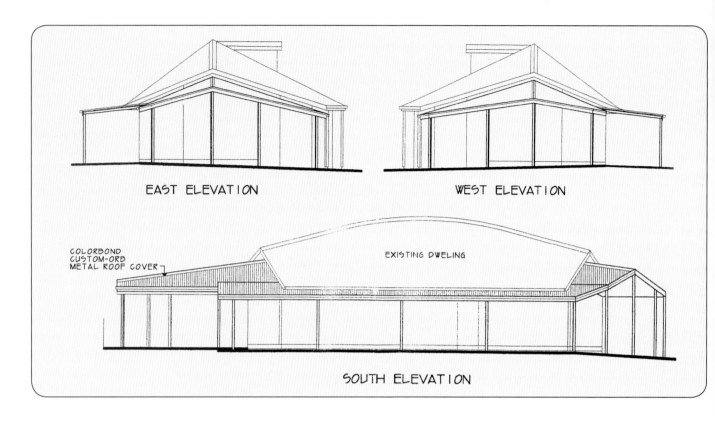

EAST ELEVATION

WEST ELEVATION

COLORBOND
CUSTOM-ORB
METAL ROOF COVER

EXISTING DWELING

SOUTH ELEVATION

Our home is a working example of permaculture, incorporating family home, office, teaching space, workshop and food processing areas. It is about 120 sq m. in size, with an additional 100 sq m. of verandah, and is built of rammed earth and timber stud walls.

Started in 1997, it achieves energy efficiency through the use of passive solar design, and low environmental impact through the careful choice of materials. An indirect benefit is that our home is a low-allergy construction.

Every material used was assessed for environmental impact. The timber framing is locally-grown radiata pine (Pinus radiata, a relatively sustainable crop) and the earth walls are made from locally-quarried gravel and clay. Although rammed earth walls are put up with the help of a bob-cat and a pneumatic rammer, the energy used is much less than that which goes into fired bricks. The end result, we believe, is more pleasant to look at and to live in.

Colorbond cladding is a relatively high energy material, though made from Australian steel, and is extremely long lasting, low maintenance and flexible—it could be bent around the unusual angles of the house. We plan to add or change windows and doors at a later time.

Permaculture emphasises the design process to achieve an environmentally-friendly result. Building our house has had a negative impact in some ways —it has caused some pollution—but our aim was to create, through good design, a building that will use very little fossil fuel and last for such a long time that it will save more energy in its lifetime than was used to build it.

We designed within constraints. Our budget was about $60,000 for the house and we had limited time—about seven months from purchasing the block to moving in. By Australian standards the house is small for two adults and three children. This is partly due to cost and also because we believe you can have 'too much house'—all that extra maintenance, the running costs and the loss of garden space—precious space in which to grow food.

We also wanted an unusual yet practical shape in addition to passive solar performance. We did most of our own design, and a local building designer (Andrew Bragg) drew plans to council standards and convinced us to include a curved roof. This is the most unique feature, something like the up-turned hull of a boat. It curves in both directions and creates the feeling of being inside an almond shell or a football rather, than a cylinder. The roof was quite a test for our carpenters but one they met with great skill. It also added an unforeseen $5,000 to our costs, though we think that was money well spent.

The curved roof is also functional. Willunga is a very windy place and we wanted a roof that was aerodynamic, that would reduce noise and minimise the risk of damage in gale force winds. The side walls of the house splay out, to direct winds away from the north-facing garden.

Apart from the unusual carpentry we stayed within budget, something helped by being 'partial owner builders'. That is, we managed the project and provided unskilled labour while employing professionals to do most of the work. We could have done more work ourselves, and collected additional second hand materials, if we had more time, but we chose not to delay completion.

Making the rammed earth walls between formwork. The previous day's wall is visible on the right

Removing the final formwork after three days' wall making

Wooden framing begins to give the house its final shape

Other main features of our permaculture-designed house are:

- a rainwater tank (3300 litres/800 gallons), gravity-fed directly to the kitchen for drinking and cooking needs

- a clerestory window to provide winter sun and plenty of natural light, and to vent out unwanted heat in summer

- a 300mm (12 inch) pipe under the foundations which draws cool air through a vented cupboard in the kitchen, reducing the size of refrigerator required. (See photo left)

- a low pressure hot water tank with solar and wood heater connections to reduce the use of the electric element. Connection pipes [green] for the wood heater are shown in foreground of photo below.

Solar provides all our hot water from late October to March or April (ie. about half the year). We don't need to run the wood heater too often to heat the house, but it heats our water for the three coolest months of the year. We do need some electricity for hot water in the cooler days of spring and autumn.

As the family grows, a sleeping platform has now been completed and we are just beginning an extension to the west. The rooms are multi-functional—for example, a bedroom became a study then reverted to being a bedroom again after the birth of our third child.

Our block is within the township and is served by electricity, mains water and sewerage. We connected to these (Willunga treats its own waste water locally, so getting approval for a composting toilet wasn't a high priority), however, the house is designed to be able to disconnect and do without these services in future, if that became desirable.

The important thing with these reticulated supplies is the quantity you use, not where they come from—high consumption of alternative energies is also unsustainable because of the energy embodied in making the photo-voltaic panels or wind turbines.

Update

We now have the benefit of living in the house for 10 years. As the children have grown into teenagers we find we need more separate spaces and have converted the car port and some of the verandah to extra living rooms.

The house has been easily warmed in winter, thanks to the winter sun, good insulation and a small amount of wood in the heater. Keeping cool on summer days has been more difficult. When the outside temperature goes over 35 degrees, there are no easy ways to keep the house cool, but the evening breezes do help.

When all else fails, it is time to head for the community pool!

A curved roof made from straight lines

The finished roof, with curve shown by low sun

"Solar provides all hot water from late October to March or April (ie. about half the year). Running the wood heater to heat the house is minimal, but it heats our water for the three coolest months of the year. Some electricity is needed for hot water in the cooler days of spring and autumn."

In autumn, the leaves have already fallen from the grape vines and peaches, to allow the sun to become the main way of heating the house

The garden

Our aim is to blend the house and garden together, with vines established on the north and north west sides for summer shade, and vegetables, herbs and fruit trees at back and front of the house.

The first important principle on our site was to save the topsoil, which was more than 300mm deep, and easily stockpiled while the building work was underway. More than 100 tonnes of loam was gained. Once the construction phase was over, local compost maker, Marty Vaher, added a truck load of his compost. As soon as spring came, we were ready to garden—with a rich, nutritious soil for the fruit trees and vegetables.

We live in an area where we can buy a wide range of fruits, available from commercial orchards (certified organic or low-spray), so we have planted trees that bear early, or late, or are experimental. For example we have a white peach that bears early but bruises easily, so it is best grown at home. We have had limited success with a banana and two avocados, although we are virtually free of frost, they need more sun.

Apples, peaches, nectarines, loquats, figs and mulberries are always successful, but need to be netted against birds and possums, who love to eat the fruit long before it is ripe!

(Garden design, soils and water systems, are also covered later in this book.)

Our house is within an unusual sub-division—the Willunga Garden Village. We are one of 20 blocks clustered around a one hectare (2.2 acres) common area. Here we have an orchard of 60 trees, an oval, swimming pool and a few wild areas.

The 'village' was inspired by Bill Mollison, who ran a permaculture course in Willunga in the early 1980s. He enthused about Village Homes in Davis, California[42] which stimulated the imagination of Ian Collett, who owned this land and wanted a sustainable way to develop it.

Ian not only chose to develop his land into an ecologically-designed community, but also set up a rammed earth building company at the same time—as well as developer, he became one of the main builders.

42 a number of websites feature Village Homes in Davis, including www.lgc.org/freepub/land_use/models/village_homes2.html   and David A. Bainbridge in www.ecocomposite.org/building/villagehomes.htm

See also Judy and Michael Corbett *Designing Sustainable Communities: Learning from Village Homes,* 2000 Island Press, Washington, D.C.

Landscape Designer: Franck Savarton & Associates.

Reconfiguring ten year-old grape vines on to a new and larger pergola

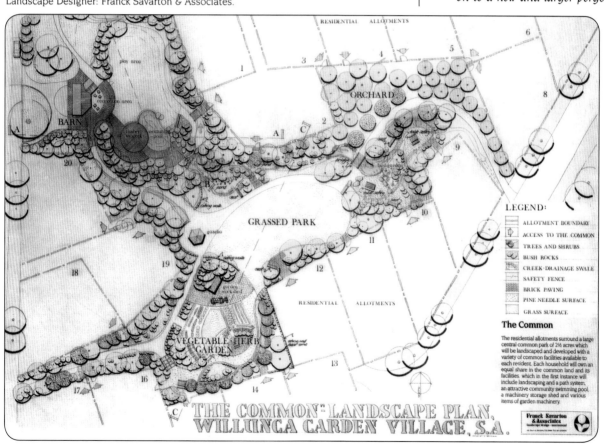

Water supply

The water to irrigate our garden cost about $100 last year and this was offset by what we grew with it, for example, 50 kilos of tomatoes. Growing food in your garden is one of the most efficient ways to use water. Had we bought certified organic tomatoes we would have paid at least $3 a kilo. In dollar terms we are ahead on this crop alone—and that's before we start to count the rest of our garden produce.

If paying the cost of water is prohibitive, or if water is not available, grow in the autumn/winter/spring only—it means you will miss out on a few crops needing lots of heat. In any area, there are times which are both warm enough and wet enough to get some crops.

Our family's approach combines many methods. We do all the basics —washing ourselves, our clothes and dishes, as well as growing a food-producing garden—but we are conscious of water use and have taken steps to save water for environmental and ethical as well as economic reasons.

It's easy to recycle water—send it down the plughole, or flush the toilet and you are recycling (usually via the sewage works and the sea). What is more important for the environment and for lower bills is to focus on reducing your need and re-using what you can. Water demand continues to rise and water is likely to get a lot more expensive. The sustainable solution is the local one.

There are ways of making more than one use of water. We keep a 10 litre bowl in the kitchen sink and a 4 litre bowl in the bathroom sink. Water that has been used for washing hands, dishes or clothes is of good enough quality for watering plants. The fig tree outside the kitchen door gets all our washing up water in summer—and there's quite a lot of washing up here!

How is your water consumption?

Measuring your water use is the first step to managing it. Our annual water use, excluding the garden, is 90,000 litres —that's for five people. That's about 60 litres or 13 gallons per day. The front-loading washing machine does about one load a day and there's both washing up and bathing as well.

In the garden we have around 300 square metres under intensive cultivation, mainly vegetables and young fruit trees. They are watered by drippers and some hand watering, plus water bucketed from the house. The garden takes about 75,000 litres a year. Our annual water bill uses the entire 125 megalitres of 'cheap' water ($50) and about $36 of 'expensive' water. This amount is easily recouped by the value of the vegetables we get from the garden. (see table of how we calculate this)

Annual water use at our home

	Litres	Cost
House	90,000	
Garden	75,000	
Total	165,000	
125,000 @ 0.40		$50
Additional litres		$36
Annual Cost		$86 plus supply charge

Water-saving techniques

There are a range of water-saving techniques, some encouraged by the water authorities and others that are more unusual and, possibly, illegal. Use your common sense—if your system leads to pools of greasy muck or floods of sewage running into your neighbour's place then they are not sustainable or safe.

In the bathroom:

The flush toilet can be a huge user of water - clean water! The water supply company goes to great lengths to clean all water (for most houses) to drinking quality standard and this potable water is then used for flushing. The alternative is 'grey water'—water that has already been used in some way and is quite suitable for flushing.[43]

When we designed our house, we included our toilet in the main bathroom. Bath and shower water is held in the bath until needed, then bucketed into the toilet bowl, reducing flushing needs by about half.

We also keep a four-litre plastic ice cream container in the bathroom sink. Whenever you run the hot tap a few litres of cool water comes out first. The four litre container just happens to be the right size to catch this cool water. It can be used for flushing or soaking dirty washing.

Urine

Urine contains much of the nitrogen and phosphorous emitted by the body and is surprisingly low in bacteria. Keeping urine separate from faeces is the important step here.[44] It's a great way to 'close the loop' and put that fertility back into your garden. Peeing near the lemon tree is a time-honoured way to do this, but it is important that the soil is damp, or covered with mulch.

If your neighbours overlook your garden, the best alternative is a bucket in the bathroom half filled with sawdust. The sawdust removes odour by soaking up the nitrogen and begins the decomposition of the sawdust. After a few months on a compost heap, the garden benefits from this so-called waste product. This is another win-win method because not only are you catching and holding fertility but you are also reducing the need to flush.

43 Dr Wendy van Dok, *The Water Efficient Garden*, covers grey water and many other useful aspects of water use and reuse. http://home.nemesis.com.au/water.

44 amongst many references see: Carol Hupping Stoner (ed.) *Goodbye to the Flush Toilet* 1977; *The Humanure Handbook*, Joe Jenkins, Jenkins Publishing; and see Cornell University's web-site, www.cals.cornell.edu/dept/compost.

Laundry

Our washing machine outflow goes into a 50mm (two inch) pipe that leads to the garden. Grey water such as this must be infiltrated into the soil immediately. If it is allowed to sit on the surface or run into a neighbour's property it becomes a health risk.

A banana circle is a handy way to soak up grey water unless you live in a frosty area where bananas won't thrive. If you live in an area with cool winters, it is necessary to be able to divert your grey water back into the mains/septic in winter—it is only useful when plants are actively growing.

What about detergent? The main problem with chemicals in soap powder comes when they are concentrated in large quantities at sewage works and then allowed into a river or the sea. It is best to avoid conventional bleaches, optical whiteners and petroleum-based ingredients.

If you are using an eco-friendly substance, the small quantities of chemicals such as phosphorous in your laundry or bath water can be used by the plants if they are healthy and growing.

An alternative is to use an ionising ball or disk, which seem to work well if clothes are not heavily soiled. Our choice is a eucalyptus liquid soap with all the ingredients listed on the container.

Two tips—

1. Solar drying of clothes contributes to their whiteness and hygiene (a good use of ultra-violet light) and doesn't contribute to greenhouse gases

2. Don't try to squeeze your washing machine water into a hosepipe—you need a larger diameter, otherwise it backs up.

In the kitchen

Use plastic bowl(s) in the sink when you wash up —you can carry the water out to a tree or grape vine. Any pieces of food or vegetable peelings will rot down and feed the trees.

We have a third tap in the kitchen, plumbed to the rainwater tank. This supplies all our cooking and drinking water and is gravity fed, therefore no problems with pumps.

Rainwater—free water?

Reticulated water makes use of energy for pumping, storage and cleaning. A recent report to the Australian Senate[45] revealed Australians use 350 litres per person per day, the second highest rate in the world, and they pay almost the lowest price for water in the world. Environmental advocate, Margaret Rainbow Web, sums it up: "Current pricing policies encourage the extravagant use of water, and one excellent way to make people aware of the need to conserve water would be to charge something approaching it's true cost. Apart from wasting a precious resource, every drop of water we take from the mains is extremely costly in terms of energy inputs, and responsible for the unnecessary generation of greenhouse gasses, because of the enormous amount of power needed for processing and pumping."[46]

Storage of water

Rain caught on your roof is 'local water'—no fossil fuel was used to get it there—and it is free, however storing it costs money. Most farms and gardens in southern coastal Australia have too much water in winter, when many plants are dormant, and too little water in summer, when plants need it most.

The two most common ways of storing the winter excess for summer use are tanks and dams.

Dams

Dams need plenty of space, lose water through evaporation and can become muddy or tinged with decaying leaves. They are fairly expensive to construct but should last indefinitely. Per litre stored, dams are much cheaper than tanks. For example, every dollar spent on a tank may store about 10 litres, but a dam costing the same price could store 1,000 times more water.

Tanks

In normal households, a small tank is needed for kitchen and drinking water. We have a tank of 3,300 litres (800 gallons), which is plumbed to a third tap in the kitchen. The gutter spout has a diversion device allowing us to choose whether we catch rain or not—the first part of a rainfall washes the roof, so it is best not to collect it.

45 Committee on the Environment (Commonwealth of Australia, December 2002).

46 Permaculture SA email discussion list, January 2003.

The emphasis is on having a small quantity of high quality water to supplement the mains supply—cooking and drinking are relatively small users of water. We probably use about 5,000 litres of rain water per year, more than the tank holds, but the tank is usually topped up every week from May to October.

Does a rainwater tank save money?

It depends how you value the water. Our tank cost $300. We purchase water at 40 cents per thousand litres, so that puts a value of $2.00 on the contents of our tank! We consider our water to be a substitute for bottled water which costs around 50 cents per litre if bought in bulk or $4 per litre in small bottles. At this price, our tank water is valued between $2,500 and $20,000!!

Once you start to think carefully about water you discover many possibilities. Each household will have different requirements and different routines—design accordingly!

You can also have a new pleasure in life—every once in a while, especially when you are really busy, relax and enjoy letting that water go down the plug hole and off to the sewage works!!

Rainwater is available at the tank for a drink, or watering the garden; while the black vertical pipe goes to the third tap in the kitchen

Tanks can be sunk partly or fully into the ground; an outdoor living area can be constructed over the top

Making a productive garden

Soil

You will probably need a lifetime, and then more, to understand soils. Begin to get a sense of the structure within the soil, and the texture—get your hands dirty! Soil comes from two places: in situ—from the breakdown of bedrock and organic matter; and from imported material—blown in, washed in, from gravity and glaciers (and from humans when we make or buy compost).

Influences on soil

Over time, the following things determine the type of soil you will have:
- parent material (the bedrock)
- climate (wet or dry, hot or cold)
- topography (the shape of the land)
- organisms (life that is active in the soil).

Soil composition

Soil is made of:
- organic matter
  (humus which is decaying biota)
- minerals (from parent material)
- air (oxygen is present)
- water
- life (biota), both visible and invisible.

Profile, structure and texture

A cross section through the soil shows the profile—the 'best' bit (the organic matter) is near the top. When you are building or gardening, be careful not to bury it!

Organic Matter

top soil (most annual plants only have roots here)

sub soil (may be mixed with rock particles; perennial plants send roots down here)

sub soil may change gradually or suddenly to bedrock

Bedrock

Composting

However good your soil, you will have to add to it to grow annual vegetables year after year. When harvesting a crop you remove nutrients, mainly from the top soil. It is only in fertile soil that vegetables thrive and resist pests and disease.

Every garden needs compost and there are many ways to make it, including worm farms, bins, heaps and chickens. You will have to experiment to find a composting method that suits. Chickens do much of the work in our garden, eating food scraps and pecking at weeds. I heap the litter in their yard in spring, and sometimes autumn. When the pile gets hot it kills off weed seeds when the temperature rises.

If you are a beginner at gardening or composting, find someone to help. There may be a local gardening or permaculture group not far away. Whichever method you choose, all your household food scraps and all the weeds and old plants from your garden are composted and returned to your garden, as is any other mulch, grass clippings or pigeon poo that you can get hold of.

Ready made compost will allow you to quickly establish a productive garden

If you have poor soils or you are just beginning, it may be worth buying in some compost or soil. Most places have compost and soil companies which are either certified as organic or use 'earth-friendly' methods of producing their materials. As before, do your research with the local permaculture or gardening group to find out who is going to sell you the 'good stuff'. There are always energy costs (ie. environmental costs) in having someone else make your compost. Best to get you own system going as soon as possible, even if it is just burying your kitchen scraps out of reach of mice and dogs.

Composting at a community garden: all weeds and old plants are composted together with sawdust and animal manures from local sources. During dry periods, these materials need additional water to get the compost process started

Resources for a productive garden

Seeds and seedings

There are now many small-scale, local producers of seedlings. Raising your own seedlings is a great idea, but if you are not ready for that, local research is needed to find a source of quality, healthy seedlings.

Once accomplished at growing your own seedlings there is a market for any excess you produce. In our area, friends and neighbours will always buy seedlings. On a larger scale, there is a great demand for certified organic seedlings.

Mulch

For the first few years of my new vegetable garden I used lots of barley and pea straw to keep down weeds and build up soil fertility. Now that the soil has improved (it contains more organic matter) and the weeds are being taken over by perennial herbs like parsley and oregano, comfrey and lemon balm, I use less imported mulch, however it is still a useful way of keeping down weeds.

Mulch emulates natural forest systems where there is always a decomposing layer of leaves and dust on the surface of the soil. Thick mulch, however, can harbour undesirable pests and can keep the soil cool in spring, when ideally you want it to warm up.

A permaculture backyard makeover: transformed from couch grass to a productive garden in a few months; first using black plastic sheets to kill the grass and then loads of mulch to improve soil and continue to suppress weeds

I let my chickens scratch through the garden to clear out the bugs in autumn and spring, before planting seedlings. Usually, I don't apply the mulch until seedlings are well established as blackbirds scratch out the seedlings while searching through the mulch.

Garden shapes

Many permaculture designs include mandala gardens and herb spirals, which illustrate the benefits of the principles of 'edge' and 'aspect'. (See *Introduction to Permaculture* and other permaculture books.) They make attractive features, however, the best shape for your vegetable garden is what suits you and your land. Although my garden started as a formal circle within a square, the fruit trees are planted randomly, and after ten years, the garden has become a forest of trees, vines and herbs. My input is much less than in the early years, vegetable production has decreased to small patches between the trees, and fruit production has increased.

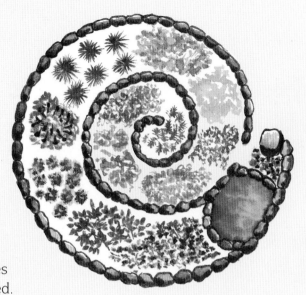

Zones and sectors

Permaculture has borrowed the zone and sector approach from other design disciplines. Zones reflect the order you impose on your garden or farm—you use the zone closest to the house for frequently visited activities (eg picking salad), and less intense ones further away (eg chicken shed, orchard).

Sectors are the directions where wild energies affect your place—hot or cold winds, flood or fire events. You need to place wind breaks, roads, ponds, and gardens accordingly.

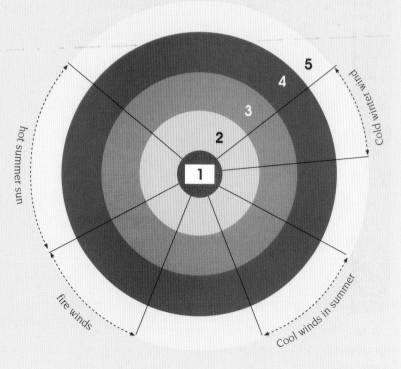

Happy eating [47]

There is a growing consensus that good nutrition is central to good health: 'you are what you eat'. But good nutrition and our relationship with food is complex. They can reflect our feelings about our self-worth, upbringing, and our relationships to wider society and the planet.

Locally produced

A local cauliflower without an organic label may well be fresher and thus better (in health terms) than an organic one that has been imported.

Fresh food loses its goodness the longer it has been picked. Supporting local farmers' markets and vegetable box schemes (such as CSA – Community Supported Agriculture) allows you to get to know local growers, this can actually influence their production methods.

The ethics of food production

Ethics, here, means the conditions under which animals and people live and work. Chicken nuggets and other chicken products from battery hens should probably carry a health warning; but even organic chickens can be intensively reared.

Apart from wild harvest of meat, lamb is the meat most likely to have been produced naturally. You may also wish to think about the conditions under which the food you buy is grown or produced. Fair Trade food outlets are one attempt to ensure a better deal for Third World producers and small farmers.

Should we eat fish?

Fish is a good source of essential oils and, from our own creek or dam, can be sustainably harvested. With the collapse of global fish stocks and the disgusting conditions under which farmed fish such as tuna and salmon is often produced, it is hard to see how eating either wild or farmed fish from beyond our own bioregion is sustainable.

47 This section was written jointly with Andrew Scott and used with permission of Liverpool School of Shiatsu (UK).

What to Eat?

Grains—whole Is best

Complex carbohydrates including whole grains (rice, wheat, oats, barley etc) and cereal products (whole-wheat bread and pasta) should form the bulk of our carbohydrate intake. These are a slow release food and are healthier for us than simple carbohydrates such as sugar.

Beware commercial white bread and flours and the products made from them. Excessive bread consumption (ie. if white bread is your main source of complex carbohydrate) should be avoided if you have a history of catarrhal conditions (bread can be mucus forming), or if you have a history of candida-related problems such as thrush or IBS (irritable bowel syndrome).

Eat more vegetables and fruit

The current recommendation is for five servings a day of vegetables and fruit (a serving is half a cup). These can be cooked or raw, fresh or frozen. Sprouts (ie. sprouted seeds, grains and pulses such as mung bean sprouts) are also good. An extra three servings per day of fruit and vegetables could reduce the risk of stroke. The high consumption of fruit and vegetables is one reason why the Mediterranean diet is so healthy. Ideally, locally grown products in season are best because this supports local producers and the food is fresher; imported or out-of-season vegetables tend to be expensive and carry high environmental costs.

Generally, it is better to scrub vegetables and fruit rather than peel them because the skins contain the most vitamins. Soaking pulses before cooking makes them more digestible.

Is organic best?

A certified organic label shows that food has been produced according to certain standards, but there is no simple answer.

Much of the organic food we eat is imported from interstate or overseas, at huge cost measured in terms of 'food miles'.[48] However,

48 The energy used in transporting the ingredients in processed food and the finished food product is measured in food miles (It could be food kilometres, but food miles sounds better.) Food miles or kilometres are a useful concept for assessing how sustainable your food purchases are.

most organic growers are improving the state of their soils and wider environment, so supporting them is worthwhile.

Eat good fat

Oils and fats are vital in a healthy diet for the essential fatty acids they contain. But generally, we eat too much of the wrong sort of oils and fats. Excess saturated fat and high cholesterol are said to harm the heart and circulatory system but there is controversy about this. It is not clear, for example, why there has been an explosion in levels of obesity and type-two diabetes in the past 20 years when 'low fat' foods have been so popular. The current advice is:

1. Eat less oils and fats and especially cut down on fried foods and high temperature roasting.

2. Eat more of the better quality oils and fats such as olive oil. The best sources of essential fatty acids from vegetable sources are nuts and seeds (including flax, sesame, walnut, sunflower, pumpkin, wheat germ, evening primrose).

Look particularly for unrefined, cold pressed oils and store these in a cool, dark place. Butter is probably healthier for you than margarine, which is a highly processed food and contains trans-fatty acids. Butter from certified organic farms is increasingly available, but remember the food miles issue.

Meat and dairy

Much commercially produced meat and dairy product come from intensively reared livestock which are routinely fed antibiotics, and in some countries, growth stimulants and other drugs, traces of which remain in the food. This problem is particularly acute in poultry production, which is why free range poultry and eggs are better. Seek out non-intensively reared meat.

If you decide to eat meat you may be surprised how little you need: just 25 grams (1 oz) of red meat a day will supply all the vitamin B12 and essential fatty acids you need. Lamb is probably the most additive-free red meat. Marinating meat in vinegar and herbs makes it more digestible. Trim the fat: choose lean varieties of red meat and consider eating white meat such as chicken or turkey if you can find unadulterated supplies.

Vegetarians and vegans

For vegetarians and vegans, variety is the key. It is possible to obtain adequate protein and to eat well without meat but only if you eat a wide variety of foods. For vegetarians, dairy products and eggs will supply protein but these are very high in fat. Vegans need to include legumes, nuts, seeds and grains as well as vegetables.

Don't forget the iron. Iron is found in two forms. Organic iron in meat, poultry and fish is easily absorbed. Inorganic iron in plant foods is less easily absorbed and its uptake by the body is affected by other foods, eaten at the same time. Organic acids and vitamin C enhance iron absorption, whole grains and tannin (e.g. in tea) inhibit iron absorption. Good sources of plant iron include legumes, whole grains, dried fruits, potato skins, dark green leafy vegetables and some nuts and seeds. Vegetarians and vegans should consider taking a vitamin C-rich fruit or drink at each meal to aid iron absorption.

Make sure adequate vitamin B12 is consumed, as it is essential for continuing health. B12 is contained in meat, eggs and dairy. At one time it was thought to be found in fermented soya products such as tempeh, seaweeds and algae. However it is now thought that this vitamin B12-like substance in these products may not be physiologically active and vegans should consider taking B12 supplements.

In terms of nutrition and health (rather than the principles of animal welfare) the issue is not whether you eat meat but whether you eat vegetables.

Stimulants

Stimulants such as coffee and alcohol are acid forming and have a particularly damaging effect on the liver. They are also addictive. Try drinking more water, tea, herb and fruit teas. A small intake of alcohol each day is healthy for some people, or simply save it for special occasions.

Eat regularly through the day, especially the complex carbohydrates which are processed and released slowly by the body. Regular meals ensure blood sugar does not fall to low levels.

Processed & sugary foods

We pay a high price for convenience foods—both financially and nutritionally. The packaging can be attractive but the quality of the highly processed contents is sometimes questionable (e.g. 'mechanically recovered meat' is an ingredient in some processed foods).

Each artificial sugar 'high' leads to a 'low', which creates further craving. The result is to disrupt the body's chemistry and create mineral imbalances and further chaotic eating. Excess sugar also tends to encourage the growth in the body of the yeast, candida albicans. Try using natural sweeteners such as honey or apple juice, but better still try to control your sweet tooth.

Beware of another common additive—MSG or Monosodium Glutamate—which is added to many processed foods as a 'flavour enhancer'. Unfortunately, for some people MSG appears to be an 'ill health enhancer' which among other things worsens catarrhal conditions. Look out for it also as 'hydrolysed vegetable protein'.

Honey production can be done on a backyard scale

Being a 'happy eater'

It is very confusing trying to find our way through today's dietary maze with the mass of conflicting advice. Being a 'happy eater' is not just a matter of what to eat in terms of foods, but also how we eat. Here are six general principles to consider, whatever the details of our diet:

1 Eat well and eat thoughtfully.
We are what we eat and what we eat is up to us. Whatever we decide, we should consider the quality of what we are eating and how it got to our plate. Is it good food prepared with love or is it adulterated junk made solely for profit?

2 Eat regularly.
It's best to make time in the day to eat, sit down and relax, especially if we tend to rush. Regular meals mean we eat less because we're less ravenous and less likely to binge. It's a way of imposing order amid the chaos of daily life.

3 Eat less, eat slowly.
Generally, we eat in a rush and overeat. By chewing our food thoroughly we not only taste it better but we become satisfied with smaller portions. Eating slower gives us a chance to reflect on our relationships with those around us and our connectedness with the planet. It's the opposite of the common 'fast food as fuel' idea.

4 Eat joyfully and without guilt.
If we are not enjoying what we are eating and we don't feel it is doing us good, why are we eating it? On the other hand we need to be flexible —a life bound by dietary prohibitions is wearing and difficult. Unless we are allergic to a food it's alright to 'sin', sometimes. Eating is often a social occasion and to refuse may cause offence.

5 Balance the five flavours.
The five flavours are: sweet, salty, sour, pungent and bitter. The idea of balance includes the principle of eating according to what is local and in season and of changing methods of cooking according to the time of year.

6 Diets don't work.
By definition, habits are hard to break. After all, food is closely linked to our personality and our view of ourselves. Dietary changes which are introduced gradually are more likely to last than big changes or prohibitions made quickly—be patient.

What is called production (goods, services) is actually consumption because the 'production' of these goods or services uses up non-renewable resources. When we look at the total impact of our individual actions at a household level, we see that in some areas we do well and in others, badly.

Personal and household strategies for sustainable living

Sustainable living begins at home. It's a constant matter of how to work with nature and how to value renewable services. This will encourage less consumption and a better quality of life—it's about change, not about doing without.

For example, I mentioned the three R's (reduce, re-use, recycle), but have you ever thought about which of them you actually do? You probably recycle. In terms of impact on the environment, however, that's the least useful of the three.

Reducing the need for an item or re-using an item is much better for the environment. Choosing to re-use a shopping bag has a greater benefit than recycling the plastic bag. Municipal recycling processes use a lot of fossil fuel to collect, melt and reform the metal, plastic and glass.

Better still is making reductions in your fossil fuel use by choosing to live near public transport (and using it), and choosing to live close to work or school, because they actually reduce the use of fossil fuels. In reality due to poor design of urban spaces, we sometimes have no choice. Even if you cannot live close to work and study today, plan towards that.

Another great step towards sustainability is to make direct use of solar power—letting winter sun come into your house, growing vines on the pergola to provide shade in summer, catching your own rain water, growing food in your own garden (and eating it) or grow in a community garden (see page 91).

Each of these activities harnesses solar power, avoiding the use of carbon-based fuels.

Conducting a personal audit examines how you use fossil fuel, alternatively what you do that relies on the sun in some way. You'll probably find you have some options for change:

• sources of food, water, building materials
• mode of transport—walk, bicycle, bus, train, car
• ways to earn an income—make it as ethical as you can.

Think about bottled water. It is pumped from underground or filtered from mains water, bottled in plastic and transported two or three times and over considerable distances before you get it. At each stage, petrol or oil is used for transport and packaging. This contributes to global warming (the 'enhanced greenhouse effect') and depletes finite reserves of fresh water. What's more, the water may cost you a dollar or more per litre (about the same as petrol).

You can run this kind of audit for any item or service you use —think about a cup of tea, an egg, or a car. It is a way of making decisions.

People are already finding environmental and economic success go hand in hand. Growers of certified organic food can't meet demand[49] and receive premium prices. Many companies around the world have an ethical and environmental approach throughout their organisation[50] and bigger companies, especially, are aware of the power of consumer boycotts. I hear that multi nationals are now keen "to be caught doing good". These are 'win-win' situations where the environment, the consumer and the business all benefit. There are impressive success stories, even at a small scale. In *Ripples in the Zambezi*, Ernesto Sirolli shows how economic development is a by-product of personal growth.[51]

At a personal level we benefit from savings derived from living within the earth's budget. Immediate beneficial side effects…an increase in quality of life and, sooner or later, a chance of survival for the human species. Time spent in the garden (growing food) and in the home (not using petrol) reduces the time needed to go out and earn money. [52]

So, think about breaking the addiction of consumerism. We are beginning to see government-funded programs to promote travel other than by using the car, including TV ads in the UK. This is a similar approach to the *Quit* (smoking) campaign. But to break an addiction, you have to first acknowledge it. What stage are you at? If you are stuck, depressed, or inspired, read the next section on 'starting points'.

Instead or simply looking at the financial cost, think about the environmental impact. Sometimes this is expressed as 'the triple bottom line', taking into account the human, community and environmental costs as well as the cash cost.

Almost every adult in the rich countries of the world owns a car, yet studies show that they spend up to 25 percent of their time earning money to pay for the car and to keep it running. Therefore, fewer cars means less stress!

49 In 2005, Australia ran out of certified organic wheat and had to import from the USA.

50 Team Poly manufacture plastic rainwater tanks and troughs and state: "Team Poly is aiming to be an industry leader by fully absorbing all emissions of CO2 emitted in the course of manufacture and distribution of its product." This is done through planting enough trees to absorb the CO2 according to the Federal Government's Greenhouse Gas Office Formula.

51 Ernesto Sirolli *Ripples in the Zambezi*, ISTP, Murdoch University, WA 1995.

52 Clive Hamilton The Australia Institute *Affluenza.* 2005 eloquently addresses the theme of knowing your true needs.

Some simple starting points

Feed yourself—sustainably

We all need food—every day. Globally, some people don't have enough while others get too much. This book is mainly for the billion or so people who do get enough (or too much) because we are the people who have time, education and affluence to allow us to write, buy and read books.

In our household, we aim to eat something from the garden every day. The food we can't grow ourselves we get through local sources wherever possible—the food co-op for dried goods, farmers' market for fresh goods or direct from other growers, often swapped for labour or our surplus pumpkins.

Like many people, our family doesn't make a high priority of gardening, but we still want to get food from it and so the garden has to rely on a few hours work a week. Our productive area is about 300m^2—less than one tenth of an acre. We don't expect to grow all we need there, however we aim to get a lot of fresh, green foods, (especially lettuce) and some potatoes and brassicas, and the herbs we use such as parsley, oregano, thyme, lemon grass, lemon balm, basil, sage etc. We have a go at the usual summer crops of tomatoes, corn, capsicums but we realise other, local commercial growers can do these better than us.

We grow more pumpkins and garlic than we need as these do well on our soil and will keep for 12 months. We are establishing strawberries as a kind of weed—planted wherever there is a bank or edge of soil.

What makes our garden so productive on so little time input is:

1. good soil—we saved the topsoil when we built the house and added lots of compost

2. minimal digging and weeding—use of straw and sawdust as mulch and dense planting to leave little room for weeds

3. lots of fruit trees—some planted, some self-seeded from our compost. As these trees become more mature they shade the veggie area, therefore our annual production is gradually becoming a perennial system

4. the use of chickens to convert food scraps and weeds into compost and eat insects like slaters (woodlice) and earwigs

5. plenty of things in flower, like nasturtiums, calendula, carrots or dill gone to seed which attract beneficial insects like hover wasps.

Feeding yourself as connection with others

Despite our urban society and lack of connection with the earth, increasing numbers of people are questioning the quality of life in a high-consuming society. Small groups of committed individuals are taking an ethical standpoint and putting positive, practical alternatives in place. Often, gardening or food supply is in some way involved though many of these initiatives are not called permaculture. That doesn't matter.

What they have in common is building with a desire to live sustainably. Robert Hart's collective name for these groups is 'The Organic Community'—people whose societies are based on mutual trust. Some of these organic communities are indigenous people living traditional lifestyles, others are groups who have come together in recent times as a response to the unhealthy condition of modern living.

The works of James Lovelock[53] (*Gaia Theory*), Fritjov Capra[54] (*The Tao of Physics* and other books) and Stephen Hawking[55] (theoretical physics at a universal scale), amongst others, show how the world is one biosphere and the molecules of the food we eat are the same as those found throughout the universe. We are part of a cosmic and interconnected system governed by rules we cannot escape. This is a modern, holistic view that is similar to that of the ancient Chinese and Indian philosophers.

Whichever of these perspectives you take, there is one common conclusion you are likely to come to—our activities have made the earth sick and that threatens our existence, as well as wiping out or threatening the existence of many other species. Even if you don't call it permaculture, the principles underlying permaculture are the prescription for that medicine.

53 James Lovelock and Lynn Margulis, *Gaia*.

54 Fritjof Capra, *The Tao of Physics*.

55 Stephen Hawking—many books.

It's natural

Permaculture uses design to link together elements in a holistic way, and uses nature as the model for sustainable systems. After all, nature has been practicing for millions of years. We can be quite certain natural systems are the best when it comes to harnessing the sun's energy ...no human design system has yet improved on it.

Staying connected

Growing something or keeping in touch with nature in some way has at least three benefits:

1. Being better informed

Permaculture and related approaches to energy accounting rest on a scientific basis such as the work of Howard and Elizabeth Odum who, between the 1960s and 2000 showed how energy, rather than cash, is the appropriate measure of sustainability. The Odums developed the concept of eMergy[56] to indicate that enERGY is EMbodied in everything we make or do.

When we throw away any item we dispose of high-quality energy (including electricity and other fossil fuels) which have been incorporated in the manufacturing process and which cannot be regained as high-quality energy. If you understand the damage created from what you are throwing away, you might feel differently about it.

2. Feeling good

Permaculture is a positive and practical antidote to the global environmental crisis and the feeling that individuals are powerless to do anything about it. We can each take small, local actions —growing food, planting trees, discussing the issues, choosing to walk or cycle instead of drive. Although small, each little choice to consume less is a vote for a better quality of life. Each little action adds to others to become something much greater.

Living and working with the seasonal changes is a healthy and generally invigorating way to enjoy life.

56 EMERGY—usually spelt in upper case, or with an upper M, to reduce the chance of it being read as energy., see p107.

3. Quality of life

You will have more with less. Many studies, including some pioneering work by Manfred Max-Neef[57] in the 1980s showed that people believed they had a better quality of life when they had fewer material possessions. This has led to alternative indicators of quality being proposed (eg. GPI—the Genuine Progress Indicator) rather than Gross Domestic Product (GDP) which measures all economic activity, regardless how destructive.

Manfred Max-Neef is a Chilean economist who has gained an international reputation for his work and writing on development alternatives. In addition to a long academic career, Max-Neef achieved an impressive minority vote when he stood as candidate in the Chilean Presidential election of 1993. He was subsequently appointed Rector of the Universidad Austral de Chile in Valdivia.

After teaching economics at the University of California (Berkeley) in the 1960s, he served as a Visiting Professor at a number of US and Latin American universities. He has worked on development projects in Latin America for the Pan-American Union, the UN Food and Agriculture Organisation and the International Labour Office.

In 1981 he wrote the book for which he is best known, *From the Outside Looking In: Experiences in Barefoot Economics*, published by the Dag Hammarskjöld Foundation, Sweden. It describes his experiences as an economist attempting to practise 'economics as if people matter' among the poor in South America. In the same year he set up in Chile the organisation CEPAUR (Centre for Development Alternatives).

CEPAUR is largely dedicated to the reorientation of development in terms of stimulating local self-reliance and satisfying fundamental human needs. More generally, it advocates a return to the human scale. CEPAUR acts as a clearing-house for information on the revitalisation and development of small and medium-sized urban and rural communities; it researches new tools, strategies and evaluative techniquest for such development, assists with projects aiming at greater local self-reliance and disseminates the results of its research and experience.

In Human Scale Development, published in 1987 in Spanish and later in English, Max-Neef and his colleagues at CEPAUR outline a new development paradigm based on a revaluation of human needs. Needs are described as existential (having, doing, being) and as axiological (values) and the things needed to satisfy them are not necessarily dependent upon, or commensurate with, the kinds or quantities of economic goods available in any given society. The book seeks to counter the logic of economics with the ethics of well-being.

"There are two separate languages now—the language of economics and the language of ecology, and they do not converge. The language of economics is attractive, and remains so, because it is politically appealing. It offers promises. It is precise, authoritative, aesthetically pleasing. Policy-makers apply the models, and if they don't work there is a tendency to conclude that it is reality that is playing tricks. The assumption is not that the models are wrong but that they must be applied with greater rigour... While the many deficiencies and limitations of the theory that supports the old paradigm must be overcome (mechanistic interpretations and inadequate indicators of well-being, among others), a theoretical body for the new paradigm must still be constructed." — Manfred Max-Neef

57 www.rightlivelihood.org/recip/max-neef.htm.

Permaculture promotes the idea of 'right livelihood'. Another phrase for this is 'earthright' [58], that is, doing the right thing by the earth.[59]

58 phrase coined by Tony Wrench and Jane Faith. See Permaculture (UK) magazine, 2000. www.permaculture.co.uk.

59 Ben Law, *The Woodland Way* Permanent Publications 2001 is a beautiful case study.

Spending money locally

Invisible structures and money

Good work

In permaculture we recognise and value work at home—both paid and unpaid—in the garden, kitchen, running a business from home and/or telecommuting… and often with children involved. Living a permaculture lifestyle doesn't always earn much cash, but it yields other income—I trade in both labour and design skills. I swap firewood, landscaping or fixing bicycles in return for accountancy, computer repair and other services and I swap permaculture design workshops in return for childcare and building materials. This is my idea of a right livelihood or an earthright way to live.

The key to this kind of income is good relationships. In the garden, we need good relationships between the soil, the plants and the animals—ecology. What I am describing is a kind of social ecology—and it only develops if you stay in one place for long enough to build those relationships. But most of this ecology cannot be seen and is difficult to measure—hence the phrase 'Invisible Structures'.

Invisible work

Much work is invisible—it has been said that some of the best leaders are those whose work is not noticed but is simply acted upon. Much permaculture work is unmeasured but it is very important. The people who fix my old car, old computer and old hi-fi sound system are some of the most important workers I know —keeping good quality equipment in use, instead of in landfill.

Growing a crop in your garden and bottling or freezing the excess will not appear in the GDP, but it remains a real contribution to the household economy.

Telecommuting is becoming more feasible. It is part of the way I work—allowing me to phone a client while working in my garden or doing the washing up, or allowing me to take in the washing when the rain starts (no electric dryer!) and then still get to work on the computer and communicate via email and the internet.

Money

I hear lots of talk about money, mostly about the lack of it. Yet each of us has thousands of dollars flowing through our hands every year. Making best use of our cash means dealing in other currencies as well—currencies such as barter, time swaps and gifts.

In our area we have a local currency called LETS[60]. Many areas have a LET System or similar. It stands for Local Exchange and Trading System, sometimes 'Local Energy Transfer System'.

Like money, it is based on an act of faith. It works because we all believe in it. Within our LETS we have about 200 people, each one a member of the 'club', with their skills listed in a directory. Its operation is simple—I do work for one person, they pay me in LETS units. I can then spend these units on a different service.

LETS doesn't pay all the bills but it helps build a sense of community and demonstrates how money works, although LETS dollars are quite the opposite of federal ones—LETS are easy to earn and harder to spend!

Most (cash) money passes quickly through a person's wallet and their local community. Money spent in a chain store usually leaves the local community quite quickly. Money spent with a local business generally stays locally. We used a local builder to help build our house—we paid him thousands of dollars, but we saw that money again and again in our local community.

Try to keep your money moving in cycles—more links = more yield (as in natural systems). The interest in community banks (such as the Bendigo Bank) is a reflection of this approach.

The 21st century version is the web-based 'freecycle' system—where you offer your unwanted goods on the internet. There's always the front gate—put your unwanted stuff on public display with a 'help yourself' sign.

LETSystems are local, non-profit exchange networks in which goods and services can be traded without the need for federal currency.

60 For info on LETS—search on the internet for you area/state and see Richard Douthwaite's book, *Short Circuit*.

Gift economy

Some people simply give things away—sometimes practising 'random acts of kindness', as the car sticker says, or sometimes in a pre-planned way. This may seem to be simply a result of an over affluent society, however gifts have been an important part of all societies.[61]

In north Wales, an area of high unemployment in the early 1990s, two men set up a 'free market' stall. Everything on offer was free. It quickly became an important way to divert 'rubbish' from going to landfill. Many people preferred to give away their unwanted goods and others wanted to take them away.   Donations were collected from any willing contributors, which more than paid for the hire of the market stall. These free market operators said: "Not a bad way to make possible a lifestyle independent of high wages and high spending!"[62]

Ethical investment

One of the biggest growth areas in finance has been in ethical investment.   Companies like Australian Ethical Investment have returned good dividends while guaranteeing that their investors money is not used for armaments, tobacco, gambling etc.

At a smaller scale, investing with friends or relatives is worth considering. Three different friends loaned us money when we were building our house. Each has been repaid and each is still a good friend! They helped us add the 'eco-features' of our house, which in turn help us live more cheaply and repay their loans.

61 Terry Leahy see www.octapod.org:8000/gifteconomy - especially "Sustainable Agriculture: A Marketing Opportunity or Impossible in the Global Capitalist Economy" and "On the Edge of Utopia: A Letter to the Green Parties".

62 The Really Free Market in Clean Slate #13, summer 1994, published by Centre for Alternative Technology, Machynlleth, Wales.

Using less fossil fuel—understanding our energy addiction

'Oil is a substance so important that it dictates world politics'—BBC Radio 4, June 2002

Conferences in Rio, (1992), Kyoto (1997) and South Africa (2002) are some bold attempts at global scale management of the impending descent down the oil mountain. But local action is needed as well. Some business and individuals are beginning to realise it makes economic sense to act as if the Kyoto Protocol was in place and to go further.

Throughout history, some civilization, somewhere in the world, has always been grasping all the resources it could get, but only in one part of the world. Access to more resources allowed that civilization to flourish, its population to grow and eventually crash, often because it destroyed its own food supply systems through unsustainable agriculture.

Today, over-exploitation occurs on a global scale. In this lies the potential for global catastrophe.

During the last 100 years, the affluent 20 per cent of the world has developed an energy addiction for concentrated doses of fossil fuels and is busy peddling the addiction to anyone else who can be seduced. We take these doses in many ways—traveling fast and frequently, eating lots of food from far-away places, filling our hours with electronic entertainment, heating or cooling our houses with electricity, and so on.

We don't want the energy as such, but we want the access it gives to a personal kind of power—a level of power that was only enjoyed by kings and emperors of former times. Of course there are great benefits to this—including, for me, being able to have time to contemplate and to sit at a computer and write.

In other words, we have had a century of free lunches but now it's time to clean up the mess and to decide to pay for the lunches in future!

Rich world levels of consumption simply cannot last:

(a) the sources of our energy are drying up—(see graph on page 11)

(b) even if we were much better at accessing solar energy, we couldn't have it in the concentrated doses we have become used to

(c) even if we found 'better' high-tech energy sources, there remain limits. For example, nuclear power appears to provide a lot of energy with little pollution. If you take into account all activities in designing and managing nuclear systems, however, they add up to huge amounts of fossil fuel (CO_2) pollution[63]. Solar panels (photovoltaic cells) also have large hidden energy costs involved in their design and production. This is not normally accounted for.

63 New Internationalist #382, page 5, "Nuclear power would make no difference to 85% of the world's climate-spoiling emissions".

While we still have plenty of energy around, it would make sense to direct quite a lot of that into designing systems (both physical and social) that can run on sustainable, solar-based power.

Permaculture's principles are founded on an understanding of these energy concepts—for a more detailed analysis, especially the work of Howard and Elizabeth Odum, see page 107.

Chainsaws can have a constructive use—taking control over our own energy supply by converting fallen branches into fuel

The right technology

The only truly sustainable technologies are those which simply gain the sun's energy and convert it without us having to do anything. An ideal example is the tree, hence permaculture's emphasis on perennial plants—forests are self sustaining. The other main natural storage is humus—the organic matter in soil—a result of leaf litter, decaying plants and the activity of earthworms.

A further way to harness the sun's energy is to build a passive solar house—see page 48.

Anything we do can be measured against a test—eg. will our house gain more solar energy in its lifetime than the fossil fuel energy we use to build it? Will the wood in our house need replacing before trees have grown sufficiently to replace those we have used? Will this book help others use less fossil fuel energy when they read it than the electricity used by the computer it is written on and the energy used to print the book?

To understand these concepts you need to investigate 'embodied energy'—which measures the total energy gone into making a product.

Transport

The most environmentally friendly approach to transport is to be where you want to be already. But if you have to move around, think of the benefits to your health and to the environment when you walk or cycle. Then consider if you could get there by public transport. If that's not available, or limited, or expensive, then consider lobbying to get better services.

The car is very useful for moving ourselves around. But for most people in the affluent world the car has become the only way of getting around. Consider the other possibilities first. If you have to drive, ask yourself if you can carry more than one person, do more than one job, or use a more fuel-efficient vehicle?

One way or another, the expectation that there will be a personal car for every journey, even a few hundred metres, is unrealistic and needs to change. Impossible? Then read on…

The resources going into making and maintaining vehicles and roads are vast, and using cars less is one of the main ways individuals can help move towards sustainability. There are alternatives, often not fully developed, but while petrol remains cheap, they remain in the 'too hard' basket.

There are plenty of alternatives, often not much developed, but while petrol remains cheap, they remain in the 'too hard' basket.

Bicycles

Bicycles are a great example of appropriate technology. They use little energy to build and recent technology makes them much lighter and more comfortable to ride. Increasingly, the addition of small electric motors makes cycling an even more viable option. On fairly flat land bicycles can easily move 100kg loads. We have often carried one or two children on a variety of trailers and child seats.

Most journeys in Australia are less than five kilometres—many are less than one kilometre. The car is almost universally used for such trips. Ironically, one of the main reasons given for not using bicycles and not letting children walk to school is the danger of the cars on the road.

This Danish-built bicycle can carry 125 kilos —about the weight of two adults

Bristol, in England, launched an internet-based 'Bike Buddies' scheme in June 2002[64]. The intention is to put experienced cyclists in touch with novices and to accompany them on their daily commute to work. In Bristol, there are over two million car trips per week of less than two miles (three kilometres). At peak hours, these trips would almost always be quicker by bike. Some places have 'walking buses' where children gather together to walk to school, needing supervision from only one adult rather than many car trips. Manchester, England, pioneered a 'safe routes to school' project in the 1980s, an idea now being adopted in other areas.

Public transport, and hybrid systems

A sustainable future requires more flexibility in our thinking. Public transport becomes possible if you can cycle and then take your bike on the bus or the train. Adding a small motor to a bicycle is another form of hybrid transport that has become quite practical with the latest technology.

I find the bicycle to be the best way to get around central Adelaide, however my town is served by buses, not trains, and I cannot take my bike on them (even though there is always room). One bus operator will carry bikes but charges twice the adult fare to do it—clearly they don't really want to. I could store a bicycle in the city and have another one at home, but meanwhile I am lobbying for an integration of the bike/bus and train system.

Other appropriate technologies

Generating electricity from wind and sun has great potential. The Brunswick/Moreland area of Melbourne has encouraged residents to put photo-voltaic cells on their roofs, so that each house makes a contribution to the grid. In Sydney, the Kogarah Town Centre has resource-efficient

Public transport becomes possible if you can cycle and then take your bike on the bus or the train

64 www.234car.com/bikebuddies.

apartments, which include rooftop photo–voltaic cells.[65]   Grid-connection technology is now readily available. This means that any household can now sell electricity to the grid when there is plenty of wind and/or sun and buy electricity from the grid when they need it. This is an example of a 'hybrid' system.

Large scale wind farms have to be located in windy areas and near transmission lines, so are often visible to many people and may be located in conservation areas. This causes controversy, but compared to fossil fuel pollution and/or nuclear power stations, many people welcome the addition of wind turbines to the landscape. Instead of seeing them as a visual pollution problem, they see them as a sustainable solution.

Even these fairly high-tech solutions have hidden—embodied—energy costs.
The most appropriate energy sources are:

• Conservation—reduce your demand for energy
• Passive solar design of buildings
• Plant based sources, grown and used locally
• Organic matter in the soil used to grow food locally.

65 See www.pacific-edge.info; and US Orion magazine for an article of rooftop wind turbines in the city, including on apartments.

Vision of a permaculture community

In towns, cities and villages around the world, people already live in communities where they talk to their neighbours, help each other, grow food together and share their social lives. These 'old fashioned' communities are quite sustainable but have been destabilised by consumer society. Others have created eco-villages and co-housing ventures where social and physical space is shared.

Not all of us need to be gardeners in this permaculture 'utopia'. If we have perishable food in our own gardens and we get everything else from local sources, then we are getting closer to living sustainably. We may only need one full-time gardener in 20, with the rest of us helping out at times of planting and peak production.

What do the rest of us do? Those who are not providing basic food needs have many other opportunities to work ethically. Think about what you'd really like to spend your time doing—it may be quite different to what you do now—and you have written your own job description.

Solutions

When we spend our money and meet our needs locally, we strengthen our community and we reduce or remove our impact on the wider environment. Robert Hart[66] is at one with permaculture when he focuses on two areas:

Bioregional design—self-reliance within your own bioregion

A bioregion is an area of land, usually defined by both natural and cultural boundaries, which provides most of the needs of the people from within that region. Typically a town or city is at the centre of a bioregion. This was the pattern of most settlement and economic development until the 20th century.

The recent focus of government on water catchment management has brought new awareness of natural boundaries, even in urban areas. Within a bioregion, everyone's basic needs should be met—transport, LETS, food, fibre and fuel supply, and some city/country links to provide a few things not easily grown in the city.

With 90 per cent of people in rich countries living in cities we need to look at urban options. One way is to see cities as farms.

66 Robert Hart, *Beyond the Forest Garden*, 1996.

Practical hands-on revegetation on the river bank

If each of our gardens were producing some food or resource, we'd have thousands of hectares under production. 'Garden agriculture' offers the joy of growing your own food and removes the need for packaging and transport and stops the loss of nutrients from another area (in the form of food).

Reafforestion

Along with the bioregional approach, we need to get a lot more trees in the ground—in both city and country areas. It's happening in many places but we are still losing old growth forests, native bush and other areas of perennial vegetation.

From tropical rainforests to dry mallee scrub, we need more trees. Organisations from farmer's federations through to conservation foundations agree that we need millions of trees. This is a global need—as we produce more and more carbon dioxide, we reduce the number of forests mopping up the surplus.

There are many marvellous forest projects happening, including innovative urban forests, but our willingness to make money from systems that destroy forests undo much of this good work. A hectare of new, small trees planted by an enthusiastic landcare group does not compensate for the loss of a complex ecosystem when an established forest is cleared. We will only reach a win-win situation when we both plant trees and minimise the removal of existing forests.[67]

With 90 per cent of people in rich countries living in cities we need to look at urban options. One way is to see cities as farms. If each of our gardens were producing some food or resource, we'd have thousands of hectares under production.

67 For musical inspiration listen to: Fay White, *Singing Landcare* (1989 – 1999)—Compact Disc, email: fwmusic@netconnect.com.au.

Commonground near Seymour, Australia. A residential community and conference centre within a low-impact passive solar building complex, surrounded by food gardens, orchards & bushland

Villages within the city and community gardens

The following examples illustrate practical solutions to our global crisis. Each helps show how bioregions can be a useful scale to meet our needs and/or to reafforest. And what better forest for a suburb than one made up of fruit trees?

Permaculture design has led directly to the creation of eco-villages. Each of these, and others incorporate permaculture principles into their design and planning requirements, allow each house to make full use of winter sunshine, water catchment, treatment and reticulation systems and opportunities for growing food in common and private areas.[68]

But permaculture communities also exist wherever a handful of people meet to exchange ideas and support each other with their own building, growing, and swapping of labour, tools and resources. These 'invisible' communities can have a big effect by meeting needs locally, and strengthening community.

Each of our suburbs can be divided into areas as small as a country town or village. Although we can go many kilometres to buy food and other goods, much of what we need is still available locally. When we shop at out local store we make a direct and strong statement of support for our local community.

"The yield is limited only by the imagination"

—Bill Mollison

68 Various guides for eco-villages and intentional communities exist, latest information on internet.

Australian examples are: Crystal Waters near Maleny in Queensland, Jarlanbah at Nimbin in NSW, Fryers Forest near Castlemaine, Vic., and the Aldinga Arts Eco-Village in South Australia.

Community gardens and city farms

The city is a farm. In towns and cities all over the world, there is a steady supply of food from suburban backyards, supplying their own table, local markets and being swapped with friends. A sustainable city needs to turn more of its land over to food production. City farms and community gardens are one way to do this.

From tiny wildlife gardens to fruit and vegetable plots on housing estates, from poly-tunnels to large city farms, these projects exist mainly in urban areas and are often a response to a lack of green space, combined with a desire to encourage strong community relationships and an awareness of gardening and farming. City farms and community gardens are often developed by local people in a voluntary capacity.

Informal learning has long been a feature of community gardens. It is the means by which gardeners learn to grow, harvest and collect the seeds of their crops. A process of gardener-teaching-gardener, it does not stop at the vegetable bed. Community gardens are social places so problem solving, conflict resolution and facilitation are add-on skills that the more enthusiastic gardeners acquire.

Many urban areas now have a city farm or community garden. There are hundreds throughout Australia, and thousands world-wide. These places are both educational and real production farms. Most community gardens include a combination of privately-run plots and public facilities. For more information see next page.

The Garden of Eden—an old railway station and its garden made in to a sustainable community garden

The Butterfly Garden

This concept is intended for use as a school produce garden and so designed to be a practical attraction and fun learning facility whilst reinforcing children's connection with nature and increasing their skills.

The plan features two caterpillars and a butterfly. The shapes present easily accessible, small individual garden plots that allow groups of children to be responsible for planning, nurturing, and harvesting produce, whether it be food or flowers, from their own site.

The covered area surrounding the storeroom can be used as an outdoor classroom, for sorting and cleaning vegetables or for an eating area. Bright coloured plastic water tanks catch roof water and are positioned to form a wind break along the back of the pergola area.

Compost bins, worm farms and chickens teach the benefits of recycling and demonstrate the importance of sustainability.

Planting a garden provides an opportunity for students to work together, learning environmental awareness and at the same time producing healthy and tasty fruit and vegetables.

Some larger community farms and gardens employ many workers whilst others are run solely by small groups of dedicated volunteers. Most are run by a management committee of local people and some are run as partnerships with local government.

Most projects provide food-growing activities, training courses, school visits, community allotments and community businesses. In addition, some provide play facilities and sports facilities, and after school and holiday schemes.

There is no typical city farm or community garden—each develops according to the local area and in response to the needs of the local community. They are places where people of all ages and from all sections of the community are welcome.

This information was taken from www.farmgarden.org.uk and www.communitygarden.org.au

The city as a dairy

How can we get other produce from our urban areas—for example, a local milk supply? The conventional dairy industry faces a lot of difficulties. It is a big system and relies heavily on fossil fuels, medication for the cows and, often leads to degradation of the land. There are now some excellent organic dairies, with lower stocking rates and homoeopathic treatments instead of hormones

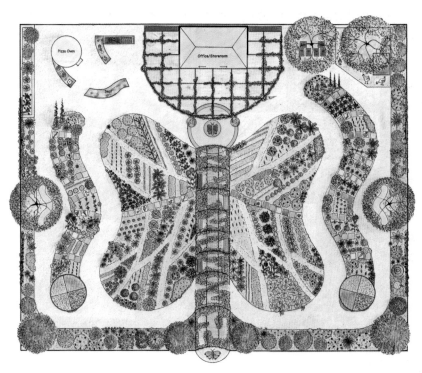

© Copyright   Landscape Designer: Virginia Sheridan

and antibiotics, but milk is still transported over huge distances between producer and consumer. The only truly sustainable milk supply is a local one. It could be achieved if:

(a) we drank less milk in total—there are good sources of calcium from nuts and seeds which can be grown in home gardens

(b) we drank goats' as well as cows' milk—goat milk is more easily digested by humans and need not taste 'goaty'. Goats can be kept in garden agriculture situations more easily than cows and can digest a wider range of foods to turn into milk

(c) we used cows to mow all the public grasslands in our cities and goats to eat up all the leaves and branches that are currently burned, shredded or thrown in a dump.

Cows' milk is better for the environment than soy 'milk', which is a highly processed product, much altered from the original soy bean. Soy products, once considered a wonder food, are now being seriously questioned from both health and environment viewpoints. The energy costs of turning a bean into milk are huge and the soy bean crop, sometimes genetically modified, is often grown in the USA, processed in Japan and sold in Australia, or sometimes the reverse! A sizeable contribution to global warming!

Scenarios such as local milk supply may seem unlikely, but imagine 10 years from now. Would you expect petrol/diesel to cost more or less than now? The world has probably already passed peak production of oil, so it is a diminishing resource. What if fuel cost three times its current price? Milk, too would have to cost more as it embodies so much oil-based energy. Perhaps the local milk example wouldn't seem so unrealistic then.

Local strategies for sustainable food supply

The following methods have been tried by permaculture-minded people with mixed success. They are trying to fill a difficult niche between self-sufficiency and big business and rely on a level of local co-operation or community business.

Food co-ops

Wholefood co-ops for non-perishable items are well established in many areas—a room in a community centre or a spare bedroom often provides the venue. A supply of grains, pulses and spreads like tahini and honey can be bought at wholesale prices, with most of the savings being passed on to the members and a small margin retained for the co-op's running costs. The advantages are minimal organisation, and substantial savings (typically 20 - 40 per cent on buying the same product in a shop). The disadvantages are that the food may get old before it's sold and the work may fall unevenly on a few people.

Perishable food co-ops often take the form of a once-a-week trip to a central market, with produce re-sold locally. The advantage is cost saving but the issues include: who decides what to buy, what happens to unsold produce and who shares the workload? These are not difficult issues to address and there are many people around with experience in how to make food co-ops work effectively.

Farmers' markets

Another idea which has taken off with great enthusiasm in Europe and North America and is gaining popularity in Australia. They are great social as well as retail occasions. The shoppers get to have a cuppa with friends and the growers often cite social contact as one of their main reasons for taking part.

At a farmers' market, the growers take their produce to a regular spot and anyone can come and buy. The advantages are lower prices, because you buy direct from the grower, but there may be unpredictable supply, due to seasonal factors.

Most farmers' markets emphasise 'local' as more important than 'organic'. Food grown locally has less environmental impact because it has travelled a shorter distance, though it may not be certified as organic.

When you buy direct from the grower, you have a chance to discuss how the crop was produced and perhaps have an influence over future growing methods.[69]

Subscription farming and food box delivery schemes

These are win-win ways of getting perishable food in a regular way. They rely on regular customers who agree to take a fixed value of fresh, organic produce each week. Subscription farming means the consumer pays a fixed weekly amount to a grower and that grower supplies a range of in-season produce, hopefully all year round.

The great advantage of this is that the grower has a guaranteed market, which should offset their extra efforts to grow a diverse range of crops. In return, the consumer has a say in what is grown and whether any chemicals are acceptable.

Food box schemes are a refinement of this system. They involve a 'middle person' who organises supplies of produce from a number of growers and/or wholesalers, and then boxes up and delivers the produce once a week. Box schemes have become very popular in northern Europe and North America since the mid-nineties, and Sydney has quite a number of these, from one-person businesses to large enterprises, where they are known as 'organic home delivery'.

69 www.farmersmarkets.org.au.

Quandongs—hardy 'bush tucker' from south-east Australia

A variation on subscription farming is 'community supported agriculture'—a wonderful idea, but rarely practised.[70] The theory is that the consumer will go to the farm to support the grower at busy times such as planting, weeding and harvesting, in return getting a good price for their food and forming a city-country link. Our local permaculture group does this in a small way, as we help each other plant and harvest significant crops (eg. garlic, potatoes, olives from 'feral' trees pressed at the local oil press, etc.)

Issues for local food systems:

Any of these systems can be set up by you and your community. Some questions always crop up, but they can (and are) soluble and shouldn't stop you trying:

- who does the work and do they expect to get paid in some way?

- is it a co-op, a private enterprise or a not-for-profit community business?

- where does the start-up capital (however small) come from?

- are you prioritising local or certified organic or uncertified but organically grown?

At present, you are unlikely to get enough food which is both grown locally and certified organic but the eco-footprint of interstate or internationally sourced food is big, whether certified organic or not. So, locally-grown and in season is the only sustainable way.

70 For more information see:
www.brisbane.foe.org.au/csa.htm.

Our family's approach is a blend of many methods. We have some perishable foods (like salads) and some staples (potatoes, corn) in our own garden. We have most of our herbs near the house—many are perennial and most take up very little space.

We aim to get all our food from within South Australia, and as much as possible from within our bio-region. We always give preference to friends' and neighbours' produce, even if it costs more —they deserve the support, the quality is good and it is the most sustainable in social and environmental terms.

Local orchards offer diverse crops from stone fruits in early summer through to apples in winter. We preserve some of this fruit by drying and bottling for off-season use. We have gaps—such as carrots (no one grows enough, so we buy them at the shop) and we have surplus —like pumpkins—which we swap with friends.

Dry food comes direct from wholesalers (bought in bulk) and honey and olive oil are purchased from neighbours. One imported luxury is custard powder—all the locally-made stuff has nasty additives like 102 and 110.

Permaculture and Feng Shui

Good design is timeless and is appreciated world wide.[71] Modern design tends to separate the house from the garden, but both feng shui and permaculture recognize the need to integrate the two. Summer shade on the sunny side of the building is important to stop a passive solar design from overheating. It can also create the right colour, quality of light and 'flow' that is required for good feng shui design.

Both permaculture and feng shui help view the world with different eyes. Both are about placing yourself, your house and your plants in the right place at the right time.

Gill Hale says: "The basis of feng shui lies in the interpretation of the natural patterns on the earth and the natural cycles of year. The closest modern system for interpreting these phenomena is permaculture which looks to care for and preserve our planet and to create systems which enable us to live and work economically in terms of finance, systems and personal energy.

In ancient times, the interpretation of astronomical and geological data was the preserve of kings and their trusty advisors. Those who held the knowledge held the power. This knowledge has, unfortunately, been hidden, lost or scattered over several disciplines in the west but it still exists if you search for it. In the east, although the preserve of the few, the knowledge has been held intact by geomancers who specialise in study of landscapes and others who prefer a more scientific approach using a large multi-ringed compass known as the Lo Pan.

The Lo Pan is merely a huge classification scheme for the universe, combining astronomy, direction and the likely effects of various landforms and planetary significance for different locations over time."

Permaculture design included the use of zones and sectors which can be seen as a simple form of the Lo Pan compass:

71 Christopher Alexander and others —*Pattern Language*, 1977.

72 Gill Hale, *The Feng Shui Garden*, 1997, Aurum Press (available from www.permaculture.co.uk); and *Feng Shui for the Southern Hemisphere*, Hermann von Essen, 2000, Axiom Publications.

"Permaculture is a form of feng shui for the modern age ... like feng shui it offers us a different view of life, co-operating with rather than dominating the natural world." [72]

—Gill Hale

Zones are the parts of your design that you control—an example being how far away something is placed and how you move from one part of your garden to another. This is the 'flow'—it doesn't have to be water, just smooth and connected like a stream.

Sectors are the 'wild' energies affecting your design—wind, sun, flood, etc. Things which can be moderated but not removed. (see page 67)

In both disciplines, there is recognition that everything is connected—best expressed by the Yin and Yang symbol.

Energy in water

We are now seeing 'flow forms' used to clean water supplies by swishing it from side to side and exposing it to ultraviolet sterilisation as it descends over a series of steps.

Callum Coates takes our understanding of water energies much further in *Living Energies*[73] In this book he covers both the life story and creations of Viktor Schauberger (1885-1958), a genius who was well ahead of his time. Like Bill Mollison, he made many observations while working in forests—for Schauberger in his native Austria—and applied these observations in many ways. Living Energies is a key text book for anyone studying water, climate, trees, springs, engineering, agriculture and energy supply.

Good placing of structures and forest make for a harmonious landscape

73 Callum Coates, *Living Energies*, Gateway Books, Bath, UK 1995.

Broadacre permaculture

Broad scale permaculture divides into two types—the 'lifestyle' landholders ('hobby farmers')[74] who want a rural living property; and commercial farmers who want to do things differently to the mainstream. The latter are often farmers who have adapted permaculture's approach to the land that they may have managed for many generations. Both types of farmers often seek organic certification, partly as a statement about their ethical attitude and partly as a marketing tool.[75]

Many people who are interested in permaculture choose a small farm or forest block, but this often means using more fossil fuel, not less, because the land has to be made productive, which takes time, energy and a lot of traveling to, usually by car. It is difficult not to drive more when you live on an acreage.

Modern commercial agriculture is a heavy user of fossil fuels. If you add energy and water costs of producing many foods, it quickly becomes clear that there is more energy used in getting the food to the table than is gained by eating it. Although modern agri-business is more conscious of the need to be 'clean and green', it still has a long way to go to be sustainable. Many agricultural industries have adopted a range of standards such as ISO 14001 and environmental management systems (EMS)

"Permaculture was originally linked to the 'back to the land' movement but has been taken up by many who have never left the land. These farmers realise there are limits to how far you can push a piece of land and they farm within those limits."

74 I have yet to find a really good term to replace 'small farm/er' or 'hobby farm/er'!

75 See the internet for organic organisations and organic success stories. In Australia, see OFA, NASAA, BFA.

Jean with heirloom corn variety in her garden at Arrow Pt, North Carolina

Areas of land once degraded by overgrazing are being returned to productivity through farm forestry

These systems help some producers get recognition of good environmental practice, but for others, they are 'greenwash'.

Permaculture's design approach can be applied at any scale. Whatever type of business and whatever size of land you manage, you need to apply permaculture principles. If you are living on the land, you always need to create your zones one and two—the areas where you provide your own fresh food from gardens and orchards. Beyond this intensive area, the strategies can vary.

Permaculture was originally linked to the 'back to the land' movement but has been taken up by many who have never left the land. These farmers realise there are limits to how far you can push a piece of land and they farm within those limits.

For example, many large farms are a combination of grazing and cropping and in a good year crops can be economically successful, especially with the addition of synthetic fertilisers. However, the loss of soil through erosion, increased salinity, and the loss of income in drought years has led some farmers to decide to graze and not crop as a way of farming the land more lightly.

The next step would be to herd kangaroo and emu instead of hard-hoofed animals, but this is beyond most western concepts of land and stock ownership and management.

Broadacre techniques

Preliminary research suggests **Natural Sequence Farming** offers a cost-effective approach for dealing with a national challenge—the management of landscapes that are prone to leach salts into water courses and to lose fertility owing to unsustainable cropping and grazing practices.

Early adopters and entrepreneurs, such as Gerry Harvey, see Natural Sequence Farming based on re-creating the core of the past to manage the present, as the future foundation for Australian farming.

http://www.nsfarming.com/

The first **Keyline** book was published in 1954. In it, P.A. Yeomans exploded the myth that it takes 1,000 years to produce an inch of topsoil. Yeomans pioneered, among other things, the use of on farm irrigation dams in Australia, as well as chisel plows and subsoil aerating rippers. Yeomans perfected a system of amplified contour ripping that controlled rainfall run off and enabled the fast flood irrigation of undulating land out with the need for terracing.

http://www.keyline.com.au/

The Food Forest [76]

The Food Forest is a multiple award-winning, permaculture farm producing 160 varieties of organically certified food. It is also a busy centre for people interested in learning skills for a sustainable way of life through work experience and short courses; and the base for a service that designs ecologically-sustainable properties.

When Annemarie and Graham Brookman bought the property in 1986 it was a bare barley paddock. Only a few towering River Red gums remained along the Gawler River from the time the Kaurna Aboriginal people camped in their shade and gathered food from the land. Today, there are thousands of native plants and a number of commercial orchards on the land. Significant wildlife species such as Brush Tailed Bettongs help the goose flock manage the orchard floor and forest. Together with myriad species of insects, birds and other creatures they form a complex and bountiful ecosystem contained within a 1.5 km (2.2 mile) predator-proof fence.

The farm covers 15 hectares, (40 acres), with organically grown fruit and nuts, wheat and vegetables, free range eggs, honey, carob beans, bush tucker, nursery plants and timber. Adding value through dehydrating, juicing, fermenting and preserving enables the Brookmans to successfully supply consumers and retailers with a diversity of products year-round.

Said Graham, "Many people have helped us develop The Food Forest with skills and knowledge handed down from previous generations, while others have come up with stunning new ideas rooted in a fusion of modern science and a commitment to sustainability. A dozen of these keen, optimistic people now teach permaculture with us in a team which harnesses university research experience, professional success stories, practical hands-on skills and a passion for the future of our landscape and the Planet. We also welcome WWOOFERs from around the globe who come to work with us and learn on the job. This is the generation who will steer humanity through the first half of this century".

76 For more information on the Food Forest, see http://www.foodforest.com.au/
and for Willing Workers on Organic Farms (WWOOF) see http://www.wwoof.com.au/.

An old stone barn, serviced by a state-of-the-art composting toilet and reedbed system, houses the learning centre for students of all ages. Other environmentally-responsible structures include a cool room, a cellar door gallery, a studio and an 'eco-gazebo' for indoor-outdoor teaching, all built using straw-bale building technology.

"The proof is in the pudding" and Annemarie and Graham have the right recipe, as environmentally designed homes, farms and backyards proliferate; as straw-bale structures pop out of the landscape; as reedbeds for domestic grey-water are popularised and as organic growing grows apace.

Strawbale workshop at The Food Forest

Graham inspecting seedset on native grasses in reveg area on the Gawler River at The Food Forest

Designing broad landscapes

Broadacre farmers, often influenced by permaculture design and certified as organic producers, are beginning to get long-overdue recognition for their careful approach to managing properties of a thousand hectares. In the Victorian Mallee, Kym Kingdon and Anthony Sheldon are integrating saltbush (as a 'living haystack') and alley cropping wheat and rye between rows of trees. Other farms in dryland Australia are droughtproofed with lucerne and windbreaks.

One dairy farmer reduced his vet's bill from $25,000 per year to around $1,000 by converting to organic milk production, which has included the use of homoeopathic treatments for the cows. Using the Albrecht approach to soil management, he increased his organic soil component by 50 per cent in just two years.

Meanwhile, 80 per cent of South Australian farmers want a moratorium on the introduction of genetically modified (GM) crops and many farmers in other states feel the same but believe they can't stop GM being imposed, even if it is only by contamination from a neighbour's property.

Most farming uses a great deal more fossil fuel energy than is contained in the food produced. Farmers usually describe their land as 'in grapes' or 'a plantation'—these are mono-cultural approaches that are quite fragile. If you only have cattle and there is a drought, or grapes and the wine market dips, or blue gums and there is an over supply of woodchips, then you have a problem. Optimal use for any area of land will be diverse.[77]

Diverse grazing

It is also possible to run different animals over same ground, as one will take certain plants and another can eat what is left. Geese, for example, will eat plantain left by other grazing animals. Possible combinations of animals are:

- cow + geese (in lush pasture)

- goat + sheep

- goat + geese in less good pasture (a dairy goat needs better grazing than a 'mowing' goat).

It is possible to 'train' animals to eat certain plants, generally by introducing them to it at a young age.

Good grazing management

For hard-footed animals, the key is to manage when and where to graze. For example, keeping animals off waterlogged ground, and avoiding 'set stocking' can make a huge difference to reducing problems of compaction. With internal fences providing 'cells', animals can be moved frequently, and grass allowed to re-grow.

If overgrazed, the roots have no chance at growing deeply, Consequently there is a short mineral cycle, not enough biomass to protect the soil, and less resistance to drought.
See illustration next page.

Grass must be allowed to grow substantially before being grazed. Land has to be managed according to type —wet/dry land, steep, etc—to avoid compaction or erosion. Good fencing is required to make this possible. This can be achieved by a combination of permanent and electric fencing.

See diagram on p105.

77 After David Holmgren, Hepburn Permaculture Design Courses 1996 onwards.

Animals for small blocks

Chickens are most common because they have so many assets, but also consider:

- ducks—less damage to plants except when small, but can create muddy areas
- geese—need green grass and access to water, but are good grazers, including kikuyu reduction, but will de-bark small trees and foul dams, especially in summer
- rabbits—eat weeds and fibrous plants which could be composted, but higher value return through the rabbit. Large rabbits (and pigeons) are a good way to produce a sustainable urban meat supply
- guinea pigs—can be free range, but need shelter from birds of prey.

Dairy animals

A dairy animal is valuable in a sustainable system. It gives a higher return and may be not much more work than a non-milking cow or goat. Consider the possibility of the 'community cow'. Working together, residents in a town can meet the cow's needs for rotational grazing and a daily input of labour for milking. They also need a diversity of plants and land to get food throughout the year to minimise the energy that goes into hay-making. Cooler/wetter parts of Australia can have year-round food for a milking animal, including tagasaste and winter growing grasses and white clover.

Training for small farmers

The 72 hour permaculture design course, is available in almost every country and is a 'must' for anyone considering buying an acreage and for anyone already living there. Many Permaculture courses are now accredited with government (eg Accredited Permaculture Training in Australia & via the WEA in the UK). Increasingly, catchment management authorities and primary industry departments of state governments offer a range of land management courses with very useful details on fencing, revegetation, pasture management and whole farm planning.

Good grazing management allows plenty of time for re-growth

Measuring total energy use— eco-footprints, life-cycles and eMergy [78]

To understand what is sustainable and what is not, we need a way of measuring both human and natural systems. Energy is a natural currency which allows us to measure and compare the value of human and natural worlds. In this way it is similar to money but more useful, because it covers more than immediate monetary costs. It is difficult, but necessary, to put a value on the services that nature provides—such as forests mopping up pollution and producing clean air. Three approaches to forming a broader measure are 'eco-footprint': Full Life-Cycle Analysis; and eMergy

Eco-footprints

Eco-footprinting is a method where our level of affluence is calculated back to how much land it takes to support our lifestyle (eg forests cut for our wood, land quarried for our road stone and concrete). In broad terms, here are some average figures per person in the following countries:

- USA—10 hectares

- Australia—7.6 ha

- Bangladesh—0.8 ha

- Me (Ian) 2.8ha (of which 1.6 is the 25 per cent of my foods that are packaged and transported)

- The world by this simple measure =1.8ha per person, (so if I only ate locally-produced food, I'd be within what's available.) [79]

Full life-cycle analysis

This is a way to measure the total impact from 'cradle to grave' of activities or products. The analysis incorporates the energy used in making a product or doing something, the running costs and the durability of materials involved. It assesses the eventual bio-degradability of the product or the ability of the materials to be reused or recycled.

78 For an in depth study see Holmgren —*Energy and eMergy – Revaluing Our World* - Collected Works 1978 - 2000.

79 You can work out your own, with a footprint calculator from www.ecofoot.org/ see www.footprintnetwork.org for national and international trends.

eMergy

Howard and Elizabeth Odum, ecologists working in the USA since the 1960s, developed a new measure which they call 'eMergy'.[80] The Odum's work has been central to the development of the permaculture concept. eMergy measures the embodied energy in every product or service, often a combination of things we can measure in dollars and others we can measure as ecological activity. The Odum's energy accounting and systems diagrams are an important tool for policy makers as they are based on the rules of the natural world, and eMergy units measure good as well as bad environmental activity.

Embodied energy

Understanding embodied energy, or 'eMergy' shows clearly that it is better to reduce the amount we consume, as it is more effective than recycling products that have already embodied a lot of energy. So, for example, it is very important to recycle any aluminium that you use as there is a huge amount of energy used in aluminium smelting. But it is more important to use less aluminium in total—where a lower eMergy product, like wood, will provide an alternative.

Additionally, consider the total energy in a project, for example, building a house. Concrete has a medium embodied energy rating but tends to be used in large quantities in modern building. So if you are building a house and are concerned about greenhouse gas emissions, reducing the concrete used is probably a higher priority than using less aluminium.

Every product contains energy, which is 'embodied' in the product. The diagram below shows how it takes 8,000 units of sunlight to produce only 1 unit of electricity. The remaining 7,999 units are dispersed as heat in the process of changing low-grade energy (light) to high-grade energy (electricity). Nobody has yet invented a more efficient way of converting sun in to high-grade energy.

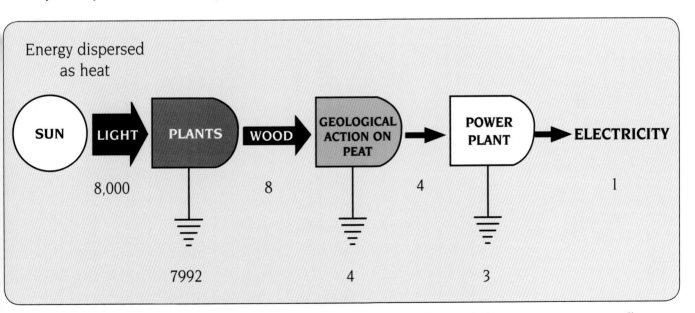

From: *Energy Basis for Man and Nature*—HT Odum and EC Odum, 2nd edition, 1981. McGraw Hill

80 HT Odum—*Environmental Accounting*, [Wiley] 1996.
Written with a capital M to avoid being mis-read as energy.

Energy laws

To understand the energy basis of everything we do, we need to know these laws of thermodynamics:

First law: The law of conservation of energy

Energy is neither created nor destroyed. The energy entering a system must be accounted for either as being stored there or as flowing out.

Second law: The law of degradation of energy.

In all processes some of the energy loses its ability to do work and is degraded in quality.

The first law means all energy is always somewhere, but most of what we use gets converted into heat and then radiates away from the earth into space.

The second law means that every time we use energy it degrades in quality. Electricity is a high-grade energy source which can, for example, run a computer. It can also heat water or a room, but that is a low-grade (inappropriate) use for the electricity as it is better done by sun or wood. Put another way, when we use electricity (a high quality energy) for heating, it quickly degrades into background radiation and is no longer useful to us.

Energy options

Sunshine is a very dilute energy form but causes no pollution (waste) when we use it to heat our home. Wood is denser in energy terms, and very good at heating a space, but it is not of a quality that can run a computer. Wood causes some pollution, but is only a problem if concentrated, for example in a valley with few breezes. With a well-designed heater, almost all the heat from burning wood is available within the house.

By comparison, burning coal or oil in a power station wastes much of the energy as heat in the power station cooling towers, then wastes more energy in transmission to your home.

This is the importance of a measure like eMergy—unless the whole picture is looked at, you don't know if you are doing environmental damage. If wood smoke pollution becomes a problem there are other options to be explored before turning to electricity for heating, which just moves the pollution to another place and increases pollution at a bigger scale. Exceptions may be places like Tasmania, where hydro power could be considered a better option for heating than wood. That depends on your attitude to flooding areas of wilderness.

Some options to improve your comfort in winter include:

• could the house be better designed (for more winter sun or thermal mass)?

• could the house be better insulated?

• does the house need to be heated as much as this? (wear more clothes, add curtains…etc).

Examples of appropriate use of external energy inputs

There are times when it may be appropriate to use the by-products of high energy society, but it is important to see them as only temporary resources to be invested, which in turn will help create long term self-sustaining systems. Some examples are:

* Waste and cheap organic materials from agriculture (hay, animal manures) or industry (paper) used to rapidly establish fertile and productive garden agricultures.

* Use of bulldozers and other heavy machinery to create well-designed permanent landforms using existing industrial capacity. This is becoming increasingly expensive as existing equipment wears out and new equipment is costly.

* Passive solar house design using existing glass manufacturing capacity to reduce future energy demands. Wholesale replacement of old housing stock would be a waste of resources.

* Native forestry with input of skilled labour in silviculture to provide structural materials with fuel as the main by-product managed on a sustainable basis. Management of natural regeneration needs more attention by permaculturists. Mixed species plantations in deforested areas to act as breeding grounds where natural and artificial selection will cull to species capable of natural regeneration.

* In rural areas wood culled from managed native forests is the most appropriate source of fuel energy. In cities super-efficient wood heaters may be appropriate to minimize pollution and use limited quantities of fuel from urban forests.

* Use of sophisticated communications and computing technology may be appropriate while these systems are available and cheap. Excessive dependence on them is unwise because of their high embodied energy, and complex and global industrial systems needed to maintain these systems.

* Settlement patterns at low densities which make best use of sunlight for heating, drying and food production and allow use of simple technologies for land-based waste disposal will be most adaptive. But infrastructure systems (buildings, roads, water supply systems) may not be able to be maintained as depreciation degrades assets and costs of replacement increases.

* Vigorous natural ecosystems capable of absorbing and using wastes (eg. overgrown gullies, weeds on unused land) should be allowed to evolve rather than using environmental technology to protect natural systems from wastes. If natural systems cannot absorb wastes then an area is overdeveloped. (eg., wood burning in cities).

Part Three: Permaculture principles

There are some underlying principles forming permaculture's natural, holistic, design-based approach to sustainability and therefore the basis for this book.

About the permaculture principles

Permaculture is a set of ethical and design principles applied in any situation—to land, housing, business, social and community development and it is vital to have an understanding of these principles to be able to assess 'what is sustainable, and where to start'.

Permaculture principles are intended to be applicable anywhere, unlike methods or strategies which vary with place, context and culture. Methods or strategies are used in this book to illustrate the principles.

There are two broad types of principles used in permaculture—ethical principles and design principles. Both draw on lessons from nature and from the collected wisdom of humans over many centuries. Each of these principles is applicable anywhere.

In the book, *Introduction to Permaculture*, Mollison and Slay list 10 Principles in addition to Ethics. These are mainly design principles, of great practical help when trying to get the right thing in the right place. Their 11th principle is a 'catch all' which deals with attitudes —the human role in sustainable design. The illustrations and text of Introduction to Permaculture are excellent and should be read in association with any other study of permaculture.

David Holmgren's, *Principles and Pathways Beyond Sustainability* brings together ethical and design principles and draws on 20 years testing these principles in the real world. Those principles provide the structure for this chapter.

In *The Designers' Manual*, Mollison outlines two basic rules about how we take responsibility: that we only use a natural resource when absolutely necessary, and if we do chose to use it, then we do so with care and sensitivity.

The principles

Permaculture principles are a combination ethical/philosophical, natural/ecological, and design principles, but there are elements of each and every one—they need to be taken as a whole. They are all inspired by 'rules' (natural laws) in nature and traditional societies that can help us design communities of plants, animals and people for self-reliance and energy efficiency. Remember that a principle must be applicable anywhere.

If you decide you want to act, then how do you know where to start, and if you are you heading in the right direction? By applying permaculture's principles we can assess all aspects of how we live —housing, transport, work, money, town planning, and social and community life, as well as food supply.

Ethical principles

Whatever version of principles you choose or refer to, there is an underlying implication—that we have the skills, resources and intelligence to design for human survival, without massive famines, wars, or destruction of what remains of our natural environment. People who are interested in permaculture promote, in some way, a transition to a global society that uses the sun's energy, converted through plants and animals, to provide enough for everybody's need.

This ethical approach sounds idealistic, but the damage, or the good, that we do is the result of millions of individual actions, past and future. The principles of permaculture help ensure individual actions are positive rather than destructive. So, although these principles at first may seem to be grand statements, they are really about guidance in our everyday life choices toward buying or growing food, moving from A to B, and putting on more clothes if you feel cold!

If it still seems too grand and idealistic, ask yourself:

(a) 'why would you want it to be any other way?'

(b) 'does each individual action move us more towards or away from sustainability?'

This section follows the order of principles used in Holmgren's book *Permaculture: Principles and Pathways Beyond Sustainability*.

David writes: "The first six principles consider systems from the bottom-up perspective of elements, organisms, and individuals. The second six principles tend to emphasise the patterns and relationships which tend to emerge by system self-organisation and co-evolution."

Where appropriate, I have related these principles to the earlier version of principles in *Introduction to Permaculture* by Bill Mollison and Rene Mia Slay. (1991).

PRINCIPLE 1—Observe and interact

To design sustainable systems, we need only observe what works, and what doesn't. Natural systems have been successful for thousands of years, and observation of wild and garden systems was central to the development of permaculture. In contrast, and despite endless Environmental Impact Statements, most modern human systems are firmly based on exploitation of fossil fuel, which cannot be sustainable. This access to concentrated fuel sources has allowed us to indulge in wasteful systems, flowing one way—from resource to waste.

Sustainable systems are those which can happen today, tomorrow and every day—indefinitely. These systems have to cycle and interact with other systems to be sustainable. To design a sustainable system can be a big task. The best way to start is at a small scale —'learn to walk before you run'. Even on a small scale, the starting point is to observe, as all around are examples of natural self-sustaining systems.

"For me, the reason to observe before interacting is to understand and then assist natural processes." [81]

Children are great observers - partly because they are closer to the ground, partly because of a childish innocence, and perhaps because they have good eyesight. You and I have images recorded in our brains of things we heard, saw, smelt, ate and touched when we were young. In designing, we need to retain a certain amount of childlike innocence in our approach and recall the patterns and details of nature's simple yet effective approach. "Those patterns and details provide us with a great repertoire of models and possibilities for the design of low energy human support systems." [82]

Permaculture design aims to be 'Imagination and Information Intensive' (rather than capital intensive or labour intensive) by using the best of old and new technologies. If we are to use intelligent design to create sustainable systems we need interaction and harmonious relationships with nature. What works? What doesn't work? Why? How much energy am I using to do this? Is there a better way? Do I need to do it at all?! Observation and interaction is the way to find out!

Information, of any type, is a powerful force. In nature, information contained in DNA manipulates and drives evolution. Information

81 Martha Hills, pers. comm.

82 Holmgren, 2002, p13.

in an old tree, animal or human is a store of wisdom. Permaculture systems draw on a wide range of information, examples being what grows where, about who has set up sustainable communities, what buildings are thermally efficient, and so on.

We need help in designing sustainable systems. Nature gives us many patterns to observe, patterns that have helped natural systems survive for a long time. David Holmgren lists the following maxims developed by permaculture teachers over the last 25 years of teaching permaculture:

• All observations are relative [83]

What works in one place, doesn't necessarily work in another. Because something is 'wrong' in one place, doesn't make it wrong everywhere. Designs and techniques vary according to many things, including the people who are designing or using the system.

• Top-down thinking, bottom-up action

This is similar to 'thinking globally, acting locally'. Because we can have a large impact at a local level, it is worthwhile to act. But how and when we act locally needs to be guided by our understanding of the big picture. For example, when water is in short supply, and rivers like the Murray are drying up, it is better to grow fruit and vegetables in your own garden and support other local growers than to buy produce from large scale irrigated farms, where water use is generally much less efficient.

• The landscape is the textbook

Permaculture has developed the concept of 'reading the landscape'. The plants, animals, humans and buildings tell us many of the things we need to know when we begin to design to change a landscape.

Careful observation of landscapes (both rural and urban) teaches us many things. This example contrasts the 'dominated landscape' (straight lines of vines) with the natural landscape on the higher slopes

83 These dot point headings are from Holmgren, 2002, p15.

We can also observe human 'landscapes' in social groups, towns, cities and cultures, and design accordingly.

• Failure is useful so long as we learn

It is ok to make mistakes, but a good idea to make mistakes at a small scale! For example, it is possible to rent a small piece of land and try growing things for a couple of years before buying land. It is a good idea to visit a piece of land at the wettest, driest, coldest and hottest times of year before buying it.

• Elegant solutions are simple, even invisible

When something works well, it is often not noticed. Many things that sustain modern life, such as reticulated water and supermarkets, are working well, and taken for granted. Unfortunately, they are only working well with a huge fossil fuel subsidy. What systems can you observe that work well and are run by the sun? Solar hot water and passive solar design are two that come to mind.

• The problem is the solution

By observation and thought, we can often find a way of solving a problem creatively. Too many insects in my garden damage plants, but free-ranging chooks through the garden once in a while turns these insects into chook food and then into eggs. The balance between insects and chooks is almost invisible, unless you are tuned into appreciating the eggs and the undamaged plants as the results of this elegant solution.

• Make the smallest intervention necessary

When we have plenty of energy and resources available, it is often easy to over-react—for example, using herbicide when a bit of mulch would do, or using the law when a chat to a neighbour would do.

• Recognise and break out of design cul-de-sacs

Although many systems get a bit better over months and years, they are often the wrong design when a bigger change comes. For example, domestic green waste is being collected and transported long distances to be cleaned up and re-imported into cities as mulch. This is an improvement on sending it straight to landfill, but unsustainable as fossil fuel energy is expensive. A low energy scenario would use the green waste close to where it is produced, at the home garden or community level.

Interaction and personal responsibility

Observation leads us to interact—to grow a crop, build a house, or set up a business or a community organisation. As we interact with a landscape or a social system, we need to observe, to see what the effects are, and to adjust our actions. Have we created or improved on a system that uses less, or no fossil fuel? Have we created a self-sustaining system which produces rather than consumes?

Gardening is always a good example. We observe the quality of food in the shops is not what we want, and we decide to grow some food. We can see from neighbours what grows well. We have some successes and some failures, and we aim to do better next time by learning from our mistakes. As sustainable systems are often quite different from how things look at the moment, we have to experiment—for example, mulch seems to benefit almost all organic gardening systems, but is 'untidy' when viewed conventionally. Bringing in mulch can bring in weeds—a new problem, and the weeds also benefit from the water you aim at the vegetables. So further thought and observation is necessary.

Leading directly from interaction comes the need to take responsibility, and this theme is developed in Principle 4—Apply Self-Regulation and Accept Feedback.

Permaculture's focus is on careful, creative design, using minimum resources to do the job. Although we aim to understand the big picture, we are only one small participant in it. We need to try our designs and learn from the mistakes—we are interacting and observing all the time. In all aspects of life, reflection is important, and helps us see solutions instead of problems. "What is needed... is the capacity to think laterally, readiness to abandon the proven and take risks, and the incentive to get to something better." [84]

Storing good quality water (for example drinking water in tanks or a dam high in the landscape) are ways of interacting and taking personal responsibility

84 Holmgren, 2002, p19.

PRINCIPLE 2—Catch and store energy

Far more sunlight is available than we use at present, though much is used by plants, and we use them, as food, timber, herbs, medicines, shelter, for aesthetic pleasure, and in many other ways. To use 'business' terminology, the earth has built up 'capital'—that is, natural resources—such as fossil fuels, by using photosynthesis to turn sunlight into plants, which in turn, have become coal, gas and oil. This has taken place over millions of years. All humans and all other life remains dependent, in some way, on sunlight and plants.

Until the last 200 years, the earth's systems were broadly in balance. However, human population growth has been made possible by us learning how to access and 'spend' the capital of the earth, and instead of using the capital to generate 'income' we have been busy making the business bankrupt.

A feast of locally-grown food sustains delegates at a permaculture conference

Fruit trees are one of nature's most successful ways of storing energy that we can use

This principle is about rebuilding the capital of the earth by setting up systems that invest in long term storage. (The next principle is about 'income'—providing sustainably for our immediate needs.) To live sustainably we have to understand the way in which natural systems catch and store energy from the environment.

Natural storage of energy

Whenever we garden, or farm, we 'capture' sunlight and convert it into food or other crops. Some of this harvest needs to be eaten immediately, other parts of it can be stored by drying, bottling, or keeping it cool. Every district has its season of abundance and season of shortage, but there are always ways of preserving excesses to see you through the hungry season.

A future 'solar economy' will harvest solar energy through use of perennial plants and through increasing organic matter in soil. Other passive systems, such as a house that gains winter sunlight for heating, or a simple solar hot water service are also examples, but many systems currently proposed as 'sustainable' (eg. photovoltaic cells) actually use huge amounts of energy in their

Until the last 200 years, the earth's systems were broadly in balance. However, human population growth has been made possible by us learning how to access and 'spend' the capital of the earth, and instead of using the capital to generate 'income' we have been busy making the business bankrupt.

research, development and construction. Wind energy, biomass from sustainably-managed systems and water provide other energy sources for permaculture systems.

Plants, water, nutrients, carbon and soil humus are all natural storages of energy that can be used sustainably, if we design effective systems. We have already seen how permaculture's focus is on design and learning from nature to create these sustainable systems. Understanding energy is central to deciding if we are living sustainably or not. Most energy we use at present comes from fossil fuels—clearly not sustainable, as they are running out rapidly.

A forest only needs natural inputs—sun, wind, rain and the animals and insects that move through it. Year after year, the trees produce nuts, seeds, fruit and its own compost that falls as leaf litter and decaying fruit. We can create perennial food systems in our gardens, parks, streets and on unused pieces of land around towns. Like natural forests, these systems become self-maintaining and we need much less annual cropping in big fields using fossil fuel to grow, transport, package and market our food.

Thinking about energy

"To move beyond the more easily understood metaphors of capitalism and financial planning, we need at least a basic understanding of energy laws and how they are the foundation for all that is possible in nature and human affairs. Understanding of these energy laws was fundamental to the development of the permaculture concept.[85]

We are used to thinking of sources of energy as fuels that are supplied to us through the economic system, but energy (in a diversity of forms) is the driving force behind all natural and human systems. Food, which we now think of as body fuel is the most important energy which people (along with all animals) catch from their environment.

Throughout the universe, energy is always spreading from centres of concentration to vacant regions where it tends to remain dispersed and diluted. In addition, energy of high quality degrades into lower quality forms thus reducing its power to affect change or do "work" in the sense that physicists and engineers use this word. This tendency to disorder and eventual death is called entropy and affects every living and non-living system.

"Although the fundamentals of this energetic view of the world are taken as given by scientists, a major disconnection between the biophysical sciences and the social sciences, most notably economics, means the energetic view has little impact on our normal understandings of value and wealth."

85 See Article 10 Development of the Permaculture Concept in David Holmgren: *Collected Writings* 1978-2000.

However, self-organising systems (primarily living ones) can capture and transform a limited proportion of energy they absorb.

This energy is then held in storages of varying form and durability for use in self-maintenance, growth and capture of more energy. This stored energy is generally higher in quality than the source from which it was derived and is thus capable of driving a wider range of processes than the original source energy.

For living systems (from single cells to homo sapiens to the whole living planet), available energy flows are mostly erratic, limited in quantity and low in quality. Living systems are "designed" to optimise the efficiency of energy transformation and storage tend to prevail through evolution...

Although the fundamentals of this energetic view of the world are taken as given by scientists, a major disconnection between the biophysical sciences and the social sciences, most notably economics, means the energetic view has little impact on our normal understandings of value and wealth."

Or put simply: "Most people are used to the drip feed supply of the supermarket culture, which gives us "reticulated food". But getting into garden culture rather than 'fridge culture' is good for all of us! Or, put simply "Grow a garden and eat from it".

Social storage of energy

'Ordinary' food in Australian shops is some of the best quality and lowest priced in the world—it is difficult for individual gardeners or food co-ops and veggie-box schemes to be able to compete. But there are many social as well as environmental benefits to this careful, local approach to your food supply. (see page 94)

We need to create bioregional communities that are self-sustaining. This doesn't mean everyone becoming self-sufficient in everything —but being able to rely on our needs being met from within our community. These needs vary from person to person, but Holmgren refers to their family's box of 'open-pollinated'[86] seeds, cellar full of preserves and large woodpile as their important storages.

In general, sustainable household energy storages are:

* **Diverse**
* **Small**
* **Dispersed**
* **Easily used**
* **Not rich or portable enough to attract much attention from thieves**

It is not only food systems that can catch and store energy - our buildings, tools and other infrastructure are an important storage. LETS (see page 81) are successful because they set out to keep energy cycling locally in the form of skills and services. Instead of paying cash, which leaks out of the local community, payment is in barter dollars, which have to be re-spent locally.

Human knowledge and social interaction at a local level meets these criteria. The friend or neighbour who can give sound advice on fixing a computer, a tool or raising children is an invaluable store of energy. The human ability to adapt will be one of the most important factors in changing to a sustainable culture.

86 seeds saved from non-hybrid sources, that will grow 'true-to-type'.

Australia's agricultural
success is based almost
entirely on introduced plants
and animals, (saved and
'shared' over generations)
which have been remarkably
successful at providing a yield
from this landscape (though
often not sustainably).

87 Holmgren 2002, p55.

PRINCIPLE 3—Obtain a yield

"If we are serious about sustainable design solutions, then we must be aiming for rewards that encourage success, growth and the replication of those solutions."[87]

So many of our actions—big and small—create waste or pollution, rather than creating a useful yield. In food production and in social systems, we need to get an immediate return for our efforts by being connected with the sources of our sustenance. This is the income that we can take while still sustaining the capital we have created and invested (principle 2). The differences are subtle but important. Riding a jet-ski is exhilarating, but this yield (exhilaration) is unsustainable. Riding a wind surfer (which can be made from local materials) is also exhilarating and can be done whenever the wind blows at no cost to the environment.

Again, the garden provides an illustration—if you are going to put energy into gardening, then why not grow something you can eat? Nature is very good at this—plants capture energy from sunlight, then grow more leaves, which in turn capture more energy. Humans save and share the best seed or breed the best animals to increase future yields. Every area of the world has some staple crop, which yields reliably and can be stored as part of an annual cycle. The world's population still depends largely on four carbohydrate staples —rice, wheat, maize and potatoes, but rich world countries don't necessarily grow their own staples any more. Instead, these countries protect themselves from shortages by using fossil fuel and market manipulation to move crops around.

At home, potatoes provide a successful staple, but I need to supplement our supply by purchasing some from local growers. Rather than turn the whole garden over to potatoes, I prefer to grow a wider range of crops, especially hardy, self seeding green foods, garlic and perennial herbs. Of the many types of lettuce I have tried, I have two varieties of lettuce that reliably self seed in my untidy garden. One is green, one red. These lettuces often self seed and don't seem to be eaten by slugs or sparrows. They still taste good after a hot, dry spell. Their hardiness and low input demands are qualities I value as well as their taste and appearance.

Australia's agricultural success is based almost entirely on introduced plants and animals, (saved and 'shared' over generations) which have been remarkably successful at providing a yield from this landscape (though often not sustainably). When we add "bush tucker", we have never had a longer 'menu' of plants and animals to choose from when designing our sustainable systems. Genetic engineering seems an unnecessary risk when you look at what is already available!

In social systems, too, we can obtain a yield while strengthening the 'capital' (a process sometimes called 'community building' or 'capacity building'.) If we join a local permaculture group, and it helps design our property, improve our business or get the social contact we need, then we are getting a yield. A group operating well gets on with the job and gets satisfaction from doing that job. Where we spend our money sends signals to producers that there is a demand. Buying organic food is a good example—unless we buy it, there is no signal to increase the production of organic food. In paying more for organic food, we are investing in maintaining the land in good condition as well as for the food itself.

"If our personal and community relationships are only based on powerful but shifting emotional benefits and we lack the experience of more practical and concrete "yields" then it is difficult to sustain and strengthen those relationships over the long term. If on the other hand we actually depend on our family, friends and relations to maintain the house, fix the car, supply our food etc we are more likely to resolve the difficulties of relationships. This truth is more obvious in rural communities where everyone understands the realities of interdependence.

This principle forces us to become more aware of the real sources of our own sustenance and well being.

In designing any system, think about what 'rewards' there will be if it works. Sustainable systems must provide a reward in the same way that our unsustainable systems do. It could be the satisfaction of harvesting and eating something you have grown, making a living from building passive solar houses, or the joy of being part of a group of people who are achieving their aims in a way that has benefits to the environment.

To obtain a yield reliably, you need to observe, and then learn when the best time is to do something, and to be flexible—things are never quite the same as they were before. 'What is a sustainable yield?' is an important question and is linked closely to the next principle—(See Principle 4. Apply Self Regulation & Accept Feedback)

Reclaimed timber is a way of getting a high quality yield from wood that might otherwise be burned or dumped

PRINCIPLE 4—Apply self-regulation and accept feedback

This principle is connected to permaculture ethics (see page 24) and to Principle 1. It is about self-reliance within your bio-region. Self-reliance is about trading with others as equals to get what you need and to help them get what they need. If we need firewood and can get it from our own property, we know if it is getting over-used. If we trade for it with someone else in our area, we can still keep tabs on whether it is being harvested sustainably. If we buy it on the 'open market', we have no idea where it came from and whether it is a sustainable harvest.

"The emphasis on personal responsibility in permaculture arises from the situation where much of the need to design for energy descent is informed by ethical principles which primarily have leverage and impact through the behaviour and actions of individuals. Despite all the talk about institutional and business ethics, it is only individual humans who can directly consider and be affected by moral concerns.

In taking personal responsibility for our needs and accepting the consequences of our own actions, we aim to change from dependent consumers of unsustainable products and services to responsible producers of appropriate wealth and value. Personal responsibility implies full awareness of the structure of our individual dependence on, and effect on local and global environment and local and global communities. Further, we need to change ourselves as our most substantial contribution to a better world.

Although many environmental activists regard this approach as politically naive and unrealistic, or simply too slow, there are sound political, historical and ecological reasons for this emphasis on personal responsibility in permaculture." [88]

Managing the earth and its resources for a global descent to sustainable levels will mean rapid change continues to happen. It will be change of a different sort. The type of change needs to be governed by the ethics of permaculture. It will require a degree of self-discipline and a certain amount of sacrifice—qualities that are not popular at a time when there is a perception that there is plenty of everything and at a time when we don't feel the consequences of our actions.

With a global information system, and plenty of lessons from history, it seems we still don't learn the lessons of history. However,

88 Holmgren 2002, p83.

our relative wealth, and availability of time and resources encourages many people to analyse what's wrong and set out to do something about it. Just thinking about managing this global change can be overwhelming, but as before, we need to start small and local. Self-regulation means setting limits on consumption and having a disciplined approach to the way we use resources. Making mistakes is alright as long as we learn from them. This feedback, if heeded, is valuable in deciding what is a sustainable system.

For example, is our gardening system taking more fossil fuel energy than it gives us in food energy, is it using up ground water that can't be replaced, is it spreading weeds into the wider environment? Intelligent design means accepting feedback when we do something, and adjusting accordingly.

Traditional societies had (and often still have) self-regulating systems, ensuring their continued survival for centuries. If they broke the rules, they soon suffered from lack of food, or other basics of life. Now that we have so much energy, it can seem like self-regulation is not needed, as we are cushioned (by fossil fuels) from the consequences of our actions.

To live within the resources of the planet is in our own self interest, and we can learn from Bill Mollison who writes, "A basic question that can be asked two ways is:

'What can I get from this land or person?' or 'What does this person or land have to give if I co-operate with them?' Of these two approaches, the former leads to war and waste, the latter to peace and plenty."

We must experiment with care—taking personal responsibility for our own small-scale lifestyles, and, more fundamentally "for our own existence and for that of our children". [89]

89 Mollison, 1988.

Hierarchy of intervention

When we do have to act to protect a crop from pests or meet our needs for shelter, a biological intervention is better than a physical one, and physical better than chemical. So one insect eating another (biological) is better than trying to find and squash the pest (physical), which is better than spraying a synthetic chemical. Grapevines for shade are better than shadecloth—they don't use petro-chemicals in manufacture and provide maximum shade at the hottest times of year and minimal shade in the winter. They may also have the added benefit of providing grapes, if the birds don't get them!

PRINCIPLE 5—Use and value renewable resources and services

When a ladybird eats aphids in our garden, we have benefited from a biological intervention, which has cost us nothing and has had no negative environmental impacts. If we use a chemical for the aphid control, we pay a cash price, and the environment suffers in terms of direct harm from the chemical and the impact from the fossil fuel energy used in making and transporting the chemical. Both Mollison (A *Designer's Manual*) and Holmgren (*Principles and Pathways*) list rules for sensible use of non-renewable resources.

So allowing the vegetable garden to become a complex ecology may reduce the immediate yield of one crop, but makes for a more sustainable garden overall. It means that the vegetable garden is like a miniature forest rather than bare, tilled soil with one crop added at a certain time of year.

If there is space, why not go for a full size forest—a food forest. If our gardens and parks were full of fruit or timber trees, many of our food and other needs, including shade and wind breaks, would be met. As well as fruit, trees can provide structural and furniture timber, fibre, natural medicines, firewood and sources of honey—a truly local source of sugar.

In spring and summer, older suburbs, when viewed from the hills, appear to have achieved urban forest status—large trees on quarter acre blocks dominate the view. An increase in food producing trees and a decrease in eucalyptus species would improve the mix, but already these trees provide most of the advantages listed above. These benefits are taken for granted, often under-used and frequently damaged by 're-development' where larger blocks are in-filled.

Energy quality

We need to limit the amount of energy our society uses in total, whether it is sourced from solar or oil-based systems, as energy is used to consume other resources. And we need to be conscious of the quality of energy we are using. Electricity is a high quality energy and can do many things from heating to running a computer. In a high energy society, it is natural to use high quality energy to do everything (as we often do when we use electricity to heat a space or water). But in moving to a sun-based economy, it is necessary to save the high quality energy for information systems (like computers) and to heat space and water using lower quality energy sources such as the sun's heat and wood.

There are many simple ways of using renewable resources—often things that our parents or grandparents would have done without thinking—like drying clothes on a washing line rather than in an electrically-powered drier. By using a tree for shade, we get a valuable service—year after year—without damage to the environment, whereas shadecloth has to be manufactured—its production causes pollution. When we cut down the tree we harvest a potentially renewable resource, as long as someone is planting at least as many trees as are felled. We also have to consider what the wood is used for. A pine tree pulped for paper may have a life of a few days or a few years. Pine used in building could last 100 years or more, and pine made into a piece of furniture could last much longer.

The tree will take at least 50 years to grow, so a greater area of trees is needed for a renewable paper supply than for building or furniture timber. Alternatively, we need to read the 'message' that we are probably using too much paper.

Sometimes fossil fuel is used to create a sustainable system. Using a bulldozer to build a dam, or cut a platform for a solar efficient house are examples, if the dam becomes a productive ecosystem and the house needs little or no fossil fuel to run once it is built.

By using renewable and biological resources, permaculture systems are managed and maintained using 'income' instead of depleting the 'capital' of non-renewables. "Renewable resources should be seen as our sources of income while non-renewable resources can be though of as capital assets. Spending our capital assets for day-to-day living is unsustainable in anyone's language."

A portable sawmill allows the renewable resource of the tree to be made into structural timber, rather than rotting in the paddock

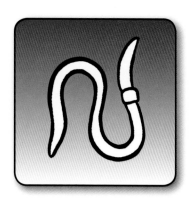

PRINCIPLE 6—Produce no waste

This principle brings together traditional values of frugality and care for material goods, the mainstream concern about pollution, and the more radical perspective that sees wastes as resources and opportunities.

Every activity, large or small, produces some waste, but if that waste then gets used by something else in the system, it is not really waste at all. When our family has breakfast, there is 'waste'—cold porridge, soggy cornflakes, bread crusts and apple cores. Not much fun for us to eat, but chooks and worms love it. By putting this "waste" in the chook run or compost heap, we regain it as improved soil, or happy chickens laying more eggs.

There are many ways to minimise pollution by designing systems that use all the outputs, but even when we get good at systems that cycle their waste, we also have to think about using less in total. This is the concept of waste minimisation, and is beginning to have some impact, as it is cheaper in cash terms, regardless of environmental considerations.

"The revolution in reduction has been greatest in industry and business because cost and competitive pressures drive rational decision-making. However, the greatest opportunities for savings from waste refusal and reduction are at the household and personal level where people often feel extravagance and waste are elements of their sense of freedom and affluence. In affluent societies new extravagant expressions of consumption develop with each generation that then degenerate into habitual norm and eventually addictive necessity in succeeding generations. The need to buy new (but poor quality clothes), the habit of throwing away half the food on the plate or leaving the lights on at night so the kids don't get scared are all behaviours which show this pattern from extravagant consumption to habitual norm to addictive necessity. Addiction to wasteful habits is a factor that has been underestimated in driving consumption by the majority and in keeping the disadvantaged poorer than they need be." [90]

Water systems can be designed to produce no waste, and water, often taken for granted, is so important it is worthy of plenty of attention. For a detailed case study, see pages 60-63.

There is a sufficiency in the world for man's need but not for man's greed.

—*Mohandas K. Gandhi*

90 Holmgren, 2002, p111 and p113.

Water—reduce and re-use

As with principle 5, (Using renewable resources) many of these actions are things that our parents or grandparents would have done without thinking.

Conservation is probably the greatest new resource available to us - hence the importance of the three R's—

1. Reduce your use of fossil fuel products

2. Reuse things where you can

3. Recycle what's left.

There are many other versions of this "R" maxim, but this one is in a particular order—reduce is the most important, reuse is second most. Recycling, often promoted as a 'green success story', is of limited value, compared with removing the need to recycle in the first place.

A trailer full of washable plates and cups plus some volunteers makes a huge difference to the amount of waste produced at catered events

PRINCIPLE 7—Design from pattern to detail

Designing is part of a process to achieve a sustainable property or product. Getting things in the right place makes the difference between sustainability or failure. Reading general patterns, and then designing in detail, is at the core of good design. This applies to a garden, farm, house or lifestyle. But going about designing anything can be confusing, or perhaps frightening, to someone who thinks of themselves as a beginner. So look at general patterns before getting down to detail.

At Willunga, in setting out to design a solar efficient home, we looked at other people's houses and read books and magazines. We considered climatic patterns, soil patterns and human habits (patterns)—our own and others in the town. In doing this, we were observing and evaluating. As a general pattern for our design, we were influenced by other owner builders in South East Australia. We aimed to take responsibility for as many parts of the process as possible, including thinking about where materials were being sourced and the environmental impact of producing those materials. We certainly planned to catch and store energy in our house and intuitively we knew that we would obtain a yield—a lovely home!

So we started off with general patterns and moved towards the detail. Only once the house was underway did some details get designed, and stage 2 was not designed in detail until after stage 1 was complete. We found the classic book A *Pattern Language*[91] helpful when working at a 'broad brush' level.

Zones and sectors, see page 67, are probably the best known way that permaculture design is applied and illustrates this principle.

Make sure you are aware of the bigger picture before working on the detail. Step back from the trees and see the whole forest! For example, before driving somewhere, consider:

* Could I walk?
* Could I cycle?
* Could someone give me a lift?
* Do I need to make the journey today?
* Do I need to go at all?

91 Christopher Alexander and others—
A *Pattern Language*, 1977, Oxford University
Press. See also Mollison—Permaculture
- A Designer's Manual, 1988, chapter 4 on
Patterns.

* If I am going to have to make this journey frequently, do I need to live closer instead, or make some other major change?

Other general patterns can include the wisdom of people—ancient and modern—and our own experience and observation. We are often designing, but we don't always realise it.

" Modernity has tended to scramble ... common sense or intuition that can order the jumble of design possibilities and options that confront us in all fields. This problem of focus on detail complexity leads to design of white elephants that are large and impressive but do not work, or juggernauts that consume all our energy and resources while always threatening to run out of control. Complex systems that work tend to evolve from simple ones which work, so finding the appropriate pattern for that design is more important than understanding all the details of the elements in the system." [92]

92 Holmgren, 2002.

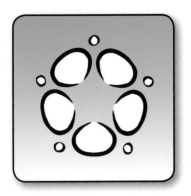

PRINCIPLE 8—Integrate rather than segregate

The connections between things are as important as the things themselves. This is shown in the Mollison principles (1991) where 'every element performs more than one function' and 'each important function is supported by many elements'. Design of farms, cities and landscapes in Australia assume there is plenty of space, and plenty of energy to move from one place to another. So we don't have much experience of integrated systems as generally we are seeing un-integrated ones.

Integrated design on a small scale includes, for example, a grapevine (an element) that provides shade, grapes and mulch (functions). Water (an important function) is supplied by more than one means: rain water tank, mains, spring, bore, dam, etc. At our home in Willunga, we can boil water by gas kettle, electric kettle or, in the winter, on the wood stove. So a power cut, or an empty gas bottle won't stop us making a cup of tea! On a larger scale, a sustainable farm may be developed by a farming family, or perhaps a group of share farmers, as a multi-functional farm, rather than as a mono-crop of pasture or grain.[93] This is especially useful as we see a growth of Community Supported Agriculture programs, which set out to provide a range of fresh foods all year round (see page 95).

Integration is also applicable to the way we design our human community—eco-villages, co-housing/cluster housing and a wide range of co-operatives and community initiatives are developed to achieve this integration. Our children's school (Willunga Waldorf School) includes fruit trees, productive gardens, and until recently, hosted a dried foods co-op—which has now moved to a high street location. Either location suits the parents, who can shop for low priced organic foods as they drop-off or pick up the children, and it suits the school because it helps (in an indirect way) to encourage enrolments.

We have to see the big picture as well as taking responsibility for small things (see Principle 4). Taking responsibility becomes possible when we have the right things in the right place.

93 The prevailing freehold land tenure remains one of the greatest impediments to the development of integrated land use in the rural Australia. Almost every large farm has some potential to include enterprises as diverse as livestock husbandry, cropping, horticulture, aquaculture, apiculture and forestry in ways that increases the productivity of all the enterprises. Unfortunately, it is uncommon for one farming family to have the skills, capital or even the cultural disposition to manage this diversity." (in Holmgren 2002).

For example, deciding to reduce your car use becomes possible only when you make decisions about living where walking, cycling, public transport, or staying at home are options.

Plants and animals are integrated in their relationship with each other—ie. they co-operate. Plant and animal systems recycle nutrients like we recycle bottles, but those natural systems are powered by the sun, whereas most recycling is powered by oil or other fossil fuels.

Integration is limited only by imagination if any waste product from one part of a system meets a need of another part eg waste food from the kitchen is no longer waste if it feeds chooks or worms. The same can apply in an organisation where something that might be rubbish can become central to another part of an organisation—as illustrated by this little story about a kettle.

At the Waldorf School, one of the old electric kettles would only warm water, not boil it. However, the food co-op needed a kettle to provide warm hand washing water—it didn't have to reach boiling point. So the solution was in the building next door, and saved the kettle from a premature trip to the dump! Larger organisations, under ever increasing pressure to be efficient, are finding this principle to be more and more important.

Without co-operation at a detailed level between families, friends and others in the community, any kind of self-reliance is impossible. "Permaculture can be seen as part of a long tradition of concepts emphasising mutualistic and symbiotic relationships over competitive and predatory ones".

"Declining energy availability (over future years) will shift the general perception of these concepts from romantic idealism to practical necessity." [94]

94 "Charles Darwin's emphasis on competitive and predatory relationships in driving evolution was based on some excellent observations of wild nature, but he was also influenced by his observations of the society around him. Early industrial England was a rapidly changing society tapping new energy sources. Predatory and competitive economic relationships were overturning previous social norms and conventions. The social Darwinists used Darwin's work to explain and justify industrial capitalism and the free market. Peter Kropotkin was one of the first of a long line of critics of the social Darwinists. He provided extensive evidence from both nature and human history on how cooperative and symbiotic relationships were at least as important as competition and predation. Kropotkin's work had a strong influence on my early thinking in developing the permaculture concept. See Kropotkin, P. Mutual Aid 1903" (in Holmgren 2002).

PRINCIPLE 9—Use small and slow solutions

Often, large scale, unsophisticated solutions have been chosen as the way to supply our basic needs, when smaller scale solutions were available and more sustainable. Smaller, slower systems are saner, and more ethical—they are better for other people and for all life-forms. For example, a home or office can be powered in many ways. The usual way is from electricity produced through large scale extraction of coal, burning the coal in large power stations, transmission along inefficient power lines and an end use in an inefficient appliance. Each stage is damaging to the environment in a number of ways, so small local systems are much better. These systems include passive solar design, (increased natural light and winter heating from the sun), and other methods such as firewood, solar hot water, wind power and photo-voltaic panels. Overall, the best systems are those that use less energy to get similar results.

The third permaculture ethic says there are limits to the amount humans can consume if we are to survive. The smaller the system, the less energy used to maintain it, and the more energy available for the yield. There is always an optimal size for any activity, but we need to remember that 'small is beautiful' [95]

'Systems should be designed to perform functions at the smallest scale that is practical and energy efficient for that function'.

A small and slow way to get to work!

'Human scale and capacity should be the yardstick for a humane, democratic and sustainable society. Whenever we do anything of a self-reliant nature from growing food, to fixing a broken appliance, to maintaining our health, we are making very powerful and effective use of this principle. Whenever we purchase from small and local business or contribute to local community and environmental issues, we are also applying this principle' (See also page 74 on local self reliance)

Many of the methods for transformation to a sustainable society are small scale and slow to develop—including the perennial plant systems we know is sustainable. Since the early days of permaculture, there has been a vision of each individual garden becoming a mini-forest, full of food and

95 EF Schumacher, *Small is Beautiful* 1973.

fibre plants. If the time and money spent by gardeners on lawns and ornamentals was re-directed to food systems, we would have a slowly developing but very important 'garden agriculture.'

Slower grown trees provide stronger timber. Slower grown food (not pumped up with extra water and nitrogen) tastes better. The slow food movement is a worldwide organisation, and the only fast thing about it is the growth of interest!

This principle also links to 'Observe' (Principle 1) where we take time to research what is going on, plan how we are to act, and follow through with determination. We spent about 4 years looking at passive solar houses, helping build other people's houses, doing designs for other houses and then turned to our own. Even then I can see how I hurried through certain parts of our own house design and those are the bits that I am not satisfied with.

Eco Villages such as Crystal Waters in Queensland, and Aldinga Arts Eco Village, in South Australia, set out to be models for whole rural and urban subdivisions, and take years in the planning and development stages. This slow speed is often frustrating and a source of conflict for the developers and residents, but shows how even a 100-house development is quite a large scale when you are not building standard off-the-shelf 'boxes'. But if we are to develop (or redevelop) suburbs and rural subdivisions for millions of people, the lessons from the apparently small eco-villages of today will be invaluable.

Start at the household level and build slowly into the wider community.

Students making garden trellis on permaculture course in Japan

PRINCIPLE 10—Use and value diversity

Pre-industrial land use and culture was very diverse. The current focus is on productivity, forcing systems to specialise and produce monocultures. Both humans and natural systems, given a chance, are interested in both diversity and productivity.

Diversity in living and built structures are important, as is diversity within species and populations, including human communities. Don't put all your eggs in one basket—diversity provides insurance!

CERES Community Environment Park in Melbourne, Victoria is a great example of permaculture-inspired diversity. CERES is 4 hectares (10 acres) of reclaimed inner city land, and is one of the most visited environmental education centres in Australia. After 20 years of dedicated effort, CERES now offers education programs, an organic farm, café, permaculture and bushfoods nursery, an energy education park, an energy efficient demonstration house, farmers' market and an annual cycle of festivals.

It is home to the Alternative Technology Centre (with a solar-powered workshop), LETS, Chook Club, Bike Club, Community Gardens and craft groups. But what makes any place like CERES is the numbers of people that come through and interact at this former dump that has now become an important social centre.

Diversity and surprising gardens

It's often said to be hard to find the time and enthusiasm to garden, but an uncontrolled and diverse garden that needs to be explored and which produces surprises like ripe strawberries or self-seeded potatoes is achievable with little time, and is more likely to attract me than a few straight rows of cabbages and leeks.

These diverse mini-food forests are also appealing to children as places to explore, and the children become the best way of harvesting small berries—not as slave labour but as unsuspecting consumers of vitamin C!

"There never were in the world two opinions alike, no more than two hairs or two grains; the most universal quality is diversity"

— *Michel de Montaigne*

Human systems also need diversity—cultural diversity, a concept of multiculturalism, as people from around the world mix, and lifestyle diversity with more intentional communities in Europe and USA—see especially the book 'Eurotopia'—a directory of over 700 intentional communities and eco-villages in Europe.[96]

"Diversity between cultivated systems reflects the unique nature of site, situation and cultural context. Diversity of structures, both living and built, is an important aspect of this principle, as is the diversity within species and populations, including human communities." [97] Diversity is a form of abundance and relates to the third ethic 'fair shares and setting limits'.

Students on an international permaculture design course, Ragmans Lane farm, Glos. UK

96 Eurotopia - *Directory of Intentional Communities and Eco-villages in Europe.* ISBN 300 00 7080X; http://www.eurotopia. de/englindex. See also Federation of Egalitarian Communities, http://www.thefec.org for USA guide.

97 Holmgren 2002, p 204.

PRINCIPLE 11—Use edges and value the marginal

It is at the edge of any thing, system or material that the interesting events take place. Edges are both productive and diverse. Be aware and make use of the edge at all scales in all systems. Maximum edge makes for maximum exchange, for example:

* The edge between a forest and a field (the 'eco-tone') is where most diversity is found.

* The urban/rural fringe around our big cities and smaller towns is where much permaculture is happening.

* The edges between academic disciplines are where exciting research is happening.

* In cities, shops are an edge—where exchange takes place.

* In the body, the lungs have a huge area of edge—another exchange place.

* In living soil, there are millions of small pockets of air and water, where the plant and the soil are engaged in exchange.

Solar houses are also an interesting aspect of edge, as we are trying to get sunshine into the house in winter and create outdoor living spaces in summer. There are few well-designed houses, so in that way they are a margin. They also form the edge between indoor and outdoor life. For many people, this is a big divide, yet living sustainably requires us to bridge that gap.

If you think of your home as 'where I am', and the environment is 'out there', (ie. separate from your life), perhaps you need a rethink. It is the design and construction of your house, and the items you consume that have a huge impact on the environment.

People who cross the edges of a number of disciplines are bridge builders and communicators, often to be found as activists in promoting permaculture and other approaches to sustainability. David Holmgren's section on the origins or permaculture at the margin (Tasmania) makes interesting reading about the edge.[98]

Humour at the edge! Graffiti is often found at social edges

98 Holmgren 2002, p235.

"People (generally from North America and Europe) sometimes ask me why I think permaculture emerged from somewhere like Tasmania. My answer is that Tasmania is a place where modernity and nature are in close proximity. It is far enough away from the sources of the dominant paradigms of society but where the benefits of modern education and relative affluence have been available for as long as anywhere else in the world. It is a place where the inspiration and lessons of nature and rural culture can be infused back into urban and intellectual culture.

Hobart, capital of Australia's second oldest and most decentralised state, is not set within some settled European landscape but clings to the foot of the wild slopes of Mt Wellington. For me it symbolises this interaction between civilisation and wilderness. From the property on the foot slopes of Mt Wellington where the permaculture concept was born in the mid 1970's it was possible to walk (or catch a bus 5 km in one direction to the city centre or the university. Five km the opposite direction on walking tracks put you on the alpine south west face of the mountain with nothing more man made than a fire trail between you and the great wilderness of SW Tasmania.[99]

Bill Mollison bridged these worlds. As the fisherman/ bushman who left school at fourteen, he went on to become a wildlife researcher, university academic, environmental activist, co-originator and teacher of permaculture around the world.

Apart from permaculture, Tasmania had the world's first green political party and was the place in Australia where the organic agriculture first grew from isolated individual farmers to a vibrant network.

Early in the 20th century, Australia was a nation where the benefits of education, political democracy and affluence were fused with exposure to the natural world and rural economy to generate an extraordinary range of scientific and technological innovation (when compared to its small population). New Zealand, with its even smaller population, has an even stronger record of innovation in science and technology.

I believe another reason for radical innovations to emerge from the fringes of the affluent and democratic world is that, in places like Tasmania, New Zealand and Denmark, the small scale of political and social institutions gives those with radical ideas, the feeling that they can make a difference. In the big cities of the great nations, the massive scale of establishment culture and institutions makes for an apathy and acceptance that the world is a bad place and cannot be changed.

In 1994 I travelled to Europe to teach permaculture and study sustainable systems both traditional and innovative. Although I saw many inspiring examples of innovation it was only in Denmark where I had the sense that the vitality and relative scale of the various "sustainable alternatives" was comparable or greater than what I was familiar with in Australia and New Zealand. In Britain and Germany, like the USA, there are a great many interesting projects, groups and individuals but not many compared to their populations."

99 Now recognised as World Heritage and the focus of the environmental battle over the Franklin River in the early 1980's.

PRINCIPLE 12—Use change constructively

"This principle has two threads: designed to make use of change in a deliberate and co-operative way, and creatively responding or adapting to large-scale system change that is beyond our control."[100]

Change is happening all the time. Gardening can help us appreciate the process of change in other parts of life. There is a direction in change. Can you influence that direction?

In earlier principles, especially 1 and 4, both the 'top-down' and the 'bottom-up' approach is discussed. At the personal, family, business and farm level, we can have some top-down control and bring about useful change—such as introducing some of the techniques described in this book, or designing others that suit you. By using techniques which promote sustainability, you are also involved in bottom-up change—sending direct and indirect messages that things can be done differently.

* * * *

In plant communities, change can be seen where there is bare soil. Nature quickly fills bare soil with whatever plants are available, to minimise the loss of soil. Areas that are overgrazed tend to become invaded by spiky plants—nature's message to keep off! Spiky plants, such as blackberry bushes, can then become a protected area where dust collects, animals defecate and tree seeds germinate, and over some time, bare land has changed to forest.

Plants provide food for animals, including humans, and in nature, and in managed farms and gardens, there is a pulsing of increased plant growth, followed by increased animal growth (eating the plants) and then a sudden reduction—at a time of catastrophe in the wild system, or harvest in the managed system. On a much larger scale, our current frenzy of consumerism can be seen as the pulse that is suddenly using up resources stored away over thousands, or millions, of years.

This process of succession can be speeded up, and often is, by human intervention—for example, planting longer term trees along with the 'pioneer species', or planting new trees before the old ones

100 Holmgren 2002, p239.

have died. Revegetation projects often plant the nitrogen fixing pioneers such as acacias and casuarinas along with the longer term eucalyptus species. Permaculture design can take advantage of these observations, by planting vegetables which will thrive for a few years between new orchard trees, or by planting new olive trees between aging almonds, which will be removed once the olives mature. But the harvest of the 'pulse' can only be sustainable if there is a long slow building phase in between. If harvests are taken too quickly, degradation occurs.

As well as plant 'pioneers', there are also human pioneers - people moving from cities to rural areas, farmers testing methods of sustainable production, owner builders, and permaculture designers. The growth of the internet, based on a myriad of home and office computers is another type of pioneering of the last decade.

"In Permaculture 1 we stated although stability was an important aspect of permaculture, evolutionary change was essential. Permaculture is about the durability of natural living systems and human culture, but this durability paradoxically depends in large measure on flexibility and change. Many stories and traditions have the theme that within the greatest stability lie the seeds of change. Science has shown us that the apparently solid and permanent is, at the cellular and atomic level, a seething mass of energy and change, similar to the way described in various spiritual traditions."[101]

Change is inevitable and can be the beginning of a new order where humans no longer treat the earth and its resources as something to consume. Change is inevitable in human systems and in eco-systems and these principles can direct us to use change in a creative way.[102]

"Permaculture is a dynamic interplay between two phases: on the one hand, sustaining life within the cycle of the seasons, and on the other, of conceptual abstraction and emotional intensity of creativity and design. I see the relationship between these two as like the pulsing relationship between stability and change. It is the steady, cyclical and humble engagement with nature that provides the sustenance for the spark of insight and integration (integrity) which, in turn, informs and transforms the practice. The first is harmonious and enduring, the second is episodic and powerful. The joyful asymmetric balance between the two express our humanity."[103]

Aboriginal Elder, Bobby Brown, discusses sustainable land management with broad acre farmer Ben Pavey on a permaculture design course in South Australia

101 Holmgren 2002, p249.

102 This principle is linked to the Introduction to Permaculture's final principle—the people-orientated or Attitudinal principle(s) and with *Permaculture - A Designer's Manual*, final chapter 'Strategies for an Alternative Nation' which develops ideas around the human role in sustainability. I highly recommend that you read them!

103 Holmgren 2002, p271.

Glossary

Active solar - a house design that uses some energy (eg a pump) to maximise its use of natural resources such as sun or wind

Autonomous house - a house that is not connected to reticulated (grid) services such as electricity and water

Bioregion(al) - an area defined by bio-physical characteristics. Ideally the people who live in the bioregion (eg a catchment or sub-catchment) get the majority of their needs met from within that bioregion

Biosphere - the outermost part of the planet—including air, land, soil and water—within which life occurs, and which biotic processes in turn alter or transform

CERES - Centre for Education and Research in Environmental Strategies, a 10-acre integrated urban sustainability project, developed over 25 years in Brunswick, Melbourne and now being replicated in other cities

City farms and community gardens - urban spaces that are both educational and productive small-scale farms. Most community gardens include a combination of privately-run garden plots and public facilities.

Eco-footprint - the amount of land that is needed to support the consumption of an individual, used as a measure of sustainability

Eco-village - a consciously designed cluster of houses (from a few to hundreds), where the principles of passive solar design and some degree of community co-operation are included

eMergy - a shorthand word for 'embodied energy', a way to measure all energy that has been used to make a product or undertake a service

Food miles (or kilometres) - the distance that an the components in an item of food has travelled before it gets to the dining table or fast food outlet. The higher the food miles, the less sustainable the product

Gaia hypothesis - an ecological theory that proposes that the living matter of planet Earth functions like a single organism

Grey water - waste water from shower, bath, sink etc., that is clean enough to irrigate trees and other plants. Grey water does not contain 'black water' from the toilet

LETS - Local Exchange Trading System—where a group of people agree to trade in a local currency

Passive solar - a design (usually of a house) that uses natural resources, such as sun and wind, for heating and cooling without using any fossil fuel in the process

Peak oil - the halfway point of all reserves of oil. Once we are past this point, production will decline, hence 'peak'. Peak Oil means not running out of oil, but running out of cheap oil

Permaculture - a designed approach to sustainable living, guided by principles, yet practical in its application

Precautionary principle - only using those resources we really need to use; living simply so that others may simply live

Subscription farming - an agreement between a farmer and a group of people to buy the farmer's produce on a regular basis, often a weekly box of fruit and vegetables

Thermal mass - the most solid part of a house, normally interior walls or floor of stone, earth, or concrete, that moderates the temperature inside the house

Third tap - an extra tap, usually at the kitchen sink, to supply rain water for drinking and cooking

WWOOFER - Willing Worker on Organic Farm—part of an international movement of volunteers of all ages.

Resources

Websites

There are thousands of local permaculture groups and many of them can be sourced through state and national organisations. These can be found on the internet. The websites below are very good starting points, but may not be 100% accurate—remember, directories are out of date as soon as they are produced.

Each of these sites has local information as well as continental and international links:

1. **International directory**: http://www.permaculture.org.uk/intgroups.asp

2. **Australia**: http://www.permacultureinternational.org/

3. **UK**: http://www.permaculture.org.uk/
   - Home of the UK permaculture network & the Permaculture Association (Britain)

4. **USA**: http://www.permaculture.net/

City farms and community gardens

1. Information on community gardens in and Australia.
   www.communitygarden.org.au - Includes a useful page on links at:
   http://www.communitygarden.org.au/links.html

2. http://www.cityfarmer.org/ (Canada)

3. www.farmgarden.org.uk/

Index